Roland's Story

Inspired by a Stroke

Roland S. Takaoka

A MEMOIR OF HOPE, HEALING AND TRANSFORMATION

Copyright © 2019 by Lynn Sanders

NOTE: This is a work of mostly fact and part fiction. Names, characters, places, have been changed, and incidents are partial products of the author's artistic flair in expression, yet all are derived from personal experience and actual events. It is intended as a documentary memoir of faith, perseverance, courage, and enlightenment.

All rights reserved. No part of this publication can be reproduced or transmitted in any form or by any means without permission in writing from the estate of Roland Takaoka or Lynn Sanders at Difference Makers Media.

Published by Difference Makers Media, LLC.
www.DifferenceMakersMedia.com

All rights reserved. Thank you for buying an authorized edition of this book and for complying with copyright laws by not reproducing, scanning or distributing any part of it in any form without permission from the Publisher. Inquiries or book purchasing can be done directly with the publisher, and should be addressed to Lynn@DifferenceMakersMedia.com.

Grateful acknowledgement is made to:
Book Covers: Rob Williams, Designer
Editing: Stephen Beale & Lynn Sanders
Interior formatting: Clark Kenyon, Camp Pope Publishing

ISBN: 978-0-9975921-5-3

Library of Congress Control Number: 2019913993

Original Manuscript: December 2012, Updated Version & Copyright: April 2019

For my beloved Barbara,
my prime example of Love and Faith.

PRAISE FOR ROLAND'S STORY

"A simply beautiful page-turner you won't be able to put down. Roland Takaoka weaves a brilliant and vulnerable journey to make you laugh, cry and appreciate the joy in adversity. A must-buy book for anyone who has suffered debilitating challenges, or knows someone who has."

– Teresa de Grosbois, International Speaker and the #1 International Bestselling author of *Mass Influence*, Founder of the Evolutionary Business Council

"*Roland's Story* is a wonderful memoir, lived by a dear friend who always looked for the best in people and helped me find the best in myself. Whether you have suffered from a stroke or experienced it as a family member or caregiver, this book will help bring healing to your mind, body and spirit!"

– David Goad, Speaker and Author

"Roland's amazing story pulled me right in. I was moved to my core by how he met his life-changing trauma with such courage, determination, and optimism. This book will inspire anyone who has ever thought about giving up."

– Debra Poneman, Founder/CEO, Yes to Success, Inc.

"From the moment I picked it up, I continued to be drawn in page after page, chapter after chapter. Roland's style of delivery gives us access to his true personality, wise and conscious, funny and accepting. His personal story is gripping, told in a way that makes us care about the

ROLAND'S STORY

protagonist and delight in his capacity to take us on a journey upon which, hopefully, we'll never have to embark.

"It's an inside story of disruption, recovery, and learning; an honest and enjoyable opportunity to be a fly on the wall during someone's most life threatening moments. This book is filled with love, laughter, and consciousness. It's easy to read, engaging, and emotionally satisfying. I highly recommend Roland's Story. *Get it and enjoy the ride."*

– Dr. Steve Taubman, Best-selling author, International speaker

"From the very beginning, I felt he was a special soul. He had a huge heart, and was so willing to listen and understand others. His only desire was to inspire. I am so happy that now he is free and can use his beautiful heart in a new way."

– Renée Mollan-Masters, Writer, Director, Producer, The Peace Train, Oregon

"I met Roland Takaoka through the 'internet' and his online LIVE show. He was someone I was immediately compelled to watch and interact with, as his sense of understanding, humor and beliefs were so close to mine ... and I really loved his smile."

– Ros Boundy, South Australia

"We quickly became good friends as we both lived our lives in a positive way. He was such a helpful, caring person. I admired him greatly for the positive way he chose to live his life, even after having three strokes and ending up in a wheelchair and unable to use the right/dominant side of his body. His book lets readers see his humor and positive outlook after his third stroke as he progressed through recovery. All readers will enjoy reading his story. It was a huge loss to many when a fourth stroke ended his life."

– Barbara Quick, Paradise, California

PRAISE FOR ROLAND'S STORY

"Roland and I co-produced a weekly show called Stroke Talk Q&A. We connected on such a deep spiritual level, and his energy as a person will live in my heart always. Roland was one of the most genuine and authentic people I'd ever met in my life. The happiest man I ever knew.

"Over the period time I got to know Roland, not only did teach me how to live stream, Roland taught me one most life changing thing – to find the genuine and authentic 'me' like he did. This truth for me was so significant it changed the course of my life forever. To you Roland, thank you for being my mentor. In the words of the most incredible man I've ever met in my life, Expand In Joy."

– Aaron Avila, Co-host of Stroke TV, California

"Roland's book is a wonder. It's as though he decided early to do away with all 'writerly' affectations and speak in his own voice. The result is the joyous testimony to a life well lived. To those of us who knew and loved him, it makes his loss more bearable."

– Burt Kempner, Award-Winning Writer/Producer/Author, Florida

"What we do know about Roland is the light you bring, the inspiration you bring to others, to the community you've created and are creating."

– Shari Alyse, Soul Ventures, Chief Inspiration Officer, The Wellness Universe, Co-Founder

"He was the epitome of an Angel or Light Bringer on this planet. I worked with Roland using frequency for months to help him reclaim some of his physical energy and taught him how to use sound to shift his body to a healthier state. Roland was always able to bring joy to what appeared to be difficult experiences in his life. He was able to dig deep and find a reason or hidden meaning to things. He would speak of them as the gifts in his life when others saw them as problems.

ROLAND'S STORY

"He was an incredible teacher and continues to touch the lives of all of those he knew on this planet through the memories that are in our hearts. His legacy lives on in each and every one of us as we live the joy that he helped us to feel through his example of 'finding the positive' in all aspects of life. Roland, I know that you are not the type to rest in peace. You are laughing, loving and blessing in your energy form! I am blessed to be part of your memory, Sweet Soul!"
–Shira Hunt, RN, CST, Owner of Vibrationally Sound, LLC, Big Island, Hawaii

"Roland Takaoka. A dear friend, a much-missed guru of 'the website' (though he still provides support, in different ways!), one of the rare men to whom I could readily and openly express, 'I love you, Man.' Someone whom I loved to make laugh, because his face lit up when that happened. Someone to whom I connected, was connected, and am connected in a trusting, caring, supportively-sharing way. A Buddy. Mahalo, Roland. I'm honored and blessed to know you. You are a part of my Ohana. Aloha."
– Capt. George S Mycroft, Website Support and Content Creator; Vibrationally Sound LLC, Honokaa, The Big Island, Hawaii

"Over the course of seven years, I had the delight of being a friend, student and therapist to Roland. He gave me each chapter of this book right after he wrote it, during the period after he had a stroke that took away his ability to move about freely or use any of his right arm or leg.

"I could not believe what I was reading! It completely and totally captured the spirit and humor that was Roland. He held me on every word, even though I was around when a lot of it was happening. He has proven to be an amazing, honest and tender writer, describing his stroke experience and rehabilitation in a touchingly, candid way. I've

PRAISE FOR ROLAND'S STORY

never ever seen anything like this. I highly recommend this book to anyone who wants to learn about the experience of stroke recovery... to anyone in healthcare... or to anyone who wants to be touched by the bottom of their soul by the beautifully, unique, loving, and so generous soul that was Roland."
– Karin Spruill, Physical Therapist, California

"While I never had the pleasure of meeting Roland in person I did have the fortunate opportunity to be interviewed by him. His passion and commitment for his work and creating a positive guest experience was memorable and deeply appreciated."
– Charmaine Hammond, Co-Founder, Raise A Dream, Victoria, BC

"I will always cherish the show he hosted, Saturday Morning Marketing Smarties, and all of the people he guided through the digital space."
– Molly Youngblood, Google Product Expert, Digital Marketing Consultant, Jacksonville, Florida

"I'm grateful that he lives through all of us. Months after his passing, he is still whispering words of love through you."
– Ty Takaoka (Roland's Son), California

"There are people who are selfless and then there is Roland. This man was here to remind us what serving others is all about as he always put people first. He was always a class act to empower others to be similar from within."
– Christopher Salem, CEO, Life & Business Strategist, CRS Group Holdings, LLC, Danbury, CT

"I gained a heartfelt sense of admiration for Roland as I accompanied him through all the obstacles he described in this book. When I first met Roland online back in 2015 in his Saturday Morning Marketing

ROLAND'S STORY

Smarties Hangout On Air, I had no idea what he had been through; Over the years we got to know each other, he shared a glimmer of his past experiences with three strokes.

"While reading this book, I was so inspired by his determination and decision to create his own reality. And what did this new reality look like in the end? He became a positive, helpful online consultant, web developer, and show host. I remember his participation in my Success Circle shows when he produced the intro music and offered his extensive knowledge and expertise to the other participants. These memories are such a contrast to what is presented in his recovery process here. To discover Roland's new reality, visit his YouTube Channel and watch a few shows: https://www.youtube.com/user/rollie1953/videos

– Lowell Ann Fulsang, Business & Career Coach-Consultant, Host of the Being Your Own CEO Success Circle, Victoria, BC, Canada

"Roland was always happy and laughing as he sat in his wheelchair. In this book, he continued to be full of joy. The book is a legacy not only for himself, but also for others who have severe injuries."

– Margherita Crystal Lotus, Healing Catalyst for Women, Stockholm, Sweden

"Loved Roland and enjoyed every minute spent in his presence. He was such a bright guiding light to so many."

– Lon McClure, Chief Technology Officer (Retired), Shelby Township, Michigan

"What a fascinating story. Roland has written a thought-provoking memoir of his personal journey after his third stroke. While some

PRAISE FOR ROLAND'S STORY

people might dwell on the challenges, Roland decides to make his experiences enlightening, inspiring and humorous. I love this book!"
– Suzy Prudden, Co-founder of Itty Bitty Publishing and Best-Selling Author, LA, California

"Roland was one of a kind. I was moved by his frank, heartfelt and optimistic journey to rehabilitate himself after his third stroke. His choice to live in joy embodies the spirit of the Keep Smiling movement!"
– Ken Rochon, Founder of The Keep Smiling Movement, Washington, DC

"Roland's heart, soul, and smile reflect through the pages bringing him back to life. What a pleasure to meet someone through his legacy who has the gift of inspiration, hope, and possibility regardless of their circumstances. A perfect read for anyone feeling conflicted with their personal circumstance! Roland's ability to laugh through life, breathed joy and love through me, to pass on through our Keep Smiling mission in spreading smiles of love and acceptance across cultures."
– Andrea Adams-Miller, International Publicist, The RED Carpet Connection & Executive Director, Keep Smiling Movement, Inc.

"Roland Takoaka was one of the most positive, upbeat people I have had the pleasure to know online. He was always giving of his time and support and we enjoyed several deep conversations around the meaning of life....always from the spirit of giving and uplifting. His warm, friendly spirit is sorely missed, and he will hold a special space in my heart for years to come."
– Virginia Parsons, Producer, Executive Women's Business Show and Media Spotlight TV, Reno, Nevada

Tribute To Roland – by Kyle Peeters (Roland's son)

"He was very calm and spiritual with a focus on positivity and balance, and I think that influenced how I saw his inner self, and really shaped the painting to be the way it is." – Kyle Peeters

AUTHOR'S NOTE

Although this book is enhanced by the colorful application of English literary license, the events are descriptions of things that really happened, however silly or absurd some of the circumstances might seem. Some of the events were contributed for the sake of the overall story by a dear friend, who actually experienced these additional occurrences first hand, and, with slight adjustments of "who and when," found their way into my story.

That being said, I look at this story as a record of true happenings, with nothing essential being invented, exaggerated or out of context. One could say, "Essentially, all events happened as they were described, with minor changes in actual dialogue and timing."

What originally began as a documentation of a challenging circumstance, evolved into a fun and inspiring expression of human nature, love, and life as it actually happened. Some morphing occurred when developing my character, who is indeed myself. I represented "him" as though he were "me" at a much younger stage of spiritual understanding, and brought him up to speed by the end of the book's chronological setting.

As for purpose, I hope this book provides inspiration, guidance and resources to:

1. Individuals who have experienced strokes
2. Those related to stroke patients – friends and family
3. Caregivers and support groups.

ROLAND'S STORY

Medical institutions are designed by those who care about people being healthy and healing. Yet, they are administered mostly by corporate entities running businesses, and therein lies a major flaw and snag in the success of national healthcare in the United States. This also produced the paradox of my own case. I benefited so much from resources granted to me, that I initially imagined were far from my reach.

Lastly, I want to convey the elements of hope and faith as they apply to healing. As a Law of Attraction enthusiast for many years, I've linked teachings that are contemporary, as well as books and resources from as far back as a century ago. I've included references as old as the major teachers, gurus, and enlightened ones that mark the hold on Divine Light and Enlightenment as the true secrets to this amazing, and often elusive, walk of life. They are all to be credited as my resources for the subjects and attitudes in this book.

For those who are dealing directly with stroke issues, the patients and their loved ones, please consider that no matter what you have experienced, or what you are told by anyone, I believe you can heal, regardless of how long it's been or how extensive the damage was.

May God bless, for, indeed, He has and does bless us, even when we forget to ask. For all that I have, and continue to receive, I am eternally grateful.

TABLE OF CONTENTS

Praise for Roland's Story — v
Author's Note — xiii
Preface — xvii

PART I IN THE HOSPITAL — 1

1. Special Delivery — 3
2. The Laugh Spasm — 7
3. The Laugh Spasm Revisited — 18
4. Menu and Other Conditions — 28
5. An Intro To Therapy — 37
6. Insights to Childbirth — 45
7. The Closest Thing To Desolation — 53
8. A Message in the Night — 60
9. I Discover What's Expected Of Me — 66
10. A Little Help Here...and There — 78
11. Good News from a Doctor? — 88

ROLAND'S STORY

PART II ADVENTURES IN REHAB   **91**

12. Review and Relief   93
13. A New Rehab and the Killer Fog   107
14. PTs, OTs, Dieticians, & Nurses   124
15. Farther Down the Rabbit Hole   137
16. A New Challenge   143
17. Night of the Banshee   151
18. Visions and Dreams   157
19. Living Proof   174
20. Shock and Disappointment   181

PART III TRANSFORMATION   **185**

21. Three Is Not Always A Charm   187
22. Daily Failure to Communicate   194
23. Engaging in a New Outlook   197

EPILOGUE   **201**

Six months later...   203
Roland's Reflections   213
A Timeless Love Story   215
Acknowledgements   231
Resources   232

PREFACE

Roland was my dearest friend, trusted business partner and an inspiration to friends, family and colleagues across the world. As unusual as it may seem, we met online through a video chat.

I was hosting an online video program, "The Difference Makers." On November 6th, 2014, I had interviewed Dale Spencer, a motivational speaker, award-winning film producer and business role model. Dale's life was transformed forever after a preventable accident at age 20. After seeing my program with Dale, Roland decided to reach out to me through an online message.

He took a risk to see if I'd be willing to talk with him, a complete stranger. I was intrigued to see why Roland liked my program.

We must have talked nonstop for an hour. I felt so comfortable with him. Just like a spark ignites a fire, our friendship was instantaneous. I know it was a soul connection. We could talk about everything. As you can guess, Roland quickly became a vital part of my business.

He not only redesigned my websites -- DifferenceMakersMedia.com and DancingWithTex.com -- but he also volunteered to serve as my technical advisor on my online shows. Although he didn't ask for payment, I often sent him money or dinner gift certificates in gratitude.

I'm grateful that Roland provided guidance for the guests on my program, 'The Difference Makers.' He was invaluable in every aspect: checking on the lighting, sound and camera angles during pre-show preparation with my online guests, monitoring the online comment

ROLAND'S STORY

stream during a show, voicing his own opinions during a program, creating thumbnail images with the guest's headshot and show title as a custom YouTube cover for the program, and adding closing slides.

The final achievement was incorporating his son's app into my website, so every show aired live through both YouTube and my own site. (Quite a tricky thing to do!) All at no charge. Besides that, Roland's calm demeanor and confidence reassured everyone, including me, when technical glitches happened.

On an everyday basis, Roland exuded warmth, compassion and joy. As he chatted with people, most never knew that he worked from his wheelchair. They didn't realize he was paralyzed on the right side of his body. They never knew he endured three strokes. All they saw from the chest up was Roland's cheerful face on the computer screen, serving others with a consistently positive attitude. He rarely mentioned his physical situation. Why would he? Other things were more important – like what he could do for YOU!

Beyond becoming an indispensable part of my program, Roland's cherished friendship meant the world to me. We could talk about anything, and spoke almost every day through Google's video hangout chats.

I learned that before his third stroke, Roland used to be a successful disc jockey and a performing guitarist in a band. He loved playing racquetball. Always eager to learn something new, Roland decided to learn about web marketing and online videos.

It's fortunate that Roland developed online skills. Being comfortable onstage, Roland was able to find a new niche for himself in the world of online media. Before long, he created "The Saturday Morning Marketing Smarties," that included a panel of knowledgeable, talented colleagues from around the world.

Imagine – each Saturday, at 11:00 am (PST), people would tune

PREFACE

in for an hour (or longer!) on their free time, to learn from Roland and his friends. The program covered a myriad of marketing topics. People typed in questions or comments and were answered promptly.

Roland also hosted an online "The Positivity Show" show. It was his goal to inspire others to feel joyful, and believe in their own potential. He also helped others build their websites, and charged very little or nothing for his time.

While pondering how to encourage more entrepreneurs, Roland decided to create an online essay contest to give away a free website. It would be a way for him to connect with more people, and help someone achieve their dream. He knew "what goes around, comes around." As it turned out, the winner of his contest was Aaron Avila, who also happened to be a stroke survivor. Aaron, like myself, felt a strong soul connection to his new 'brother,' and their relationship grew.

Together, Roland and Aaron began co-hosting the online program, "Stroke TV," with the ultimate goal of encouraging stroke survivors to speak up, share their stories and believe in themselves. Stroke survivors started showing up. To date, there are over 3,000 followers on this channel.

Whenever someone needed a listening ear, Roland would be there. He knew that while our bodies have a finite time on earth, our spirit lives on.

Roland's Story: Inspired By A Stroke does more than capture the life-changing event of Roland's experiences and recuperation from a stroke. His journey reflects that even in the most challenging of circumstances, we choose our attitude. He reinforces the powerful message, "Belief becomes reality." And he demonstrates what can happen when we believe in ourselves. He writes just as he talks, with an irresistible cheerfulness.

I used to wonder how Roland could stay so upbeat. He told me

ROLAND'S STORY

that being positive was simply a choice. Roland and I recognized a higher reason behind significant events or people who come into our lives. We felt we were meant to be connected, and I know he was my soul brother.

So, imagine there is a Higher reason why you're reading these words now. Perhaps you'll discover something in this book that touches your soul deeply. Maybe those insights will propel you to move forward. Or, Roland's Story could guide you in finding peace as you deal with your own situation. Whatever the reason, I'm glad you're here. We're now connected in spirit across the page.

It was my greatest joy to meet Roland and his wife, Barbara Peeters, when my husband Joel and I traveled on three different trips to California. Seeing Roland in person felt like a reunion with a long-time friend. We knew each other so well. There was nothing better than giving Roland and Barbara a hug in person. It was total joy.

Over time, after many deep conversations with Roland, I got motivated one day to record an interview with Roland himself. How glad I am for that interview! It's a precious treasure. A moment in time where you can experience Roland's natural, upbeat personality. Check it out: http://bit.ly/DM-Roland

Roland's community of friends continues staying in touch with one another. "Stroke TV" attracts a growing crowd of followers, led by Roland's dedicated soul brother, Aaron Avila and his new co-host, Jerry Wald. It's wonderful to see the remarkable programs produced by "Stroke TV," as a live-streaming broadcast. (Find them on YouTube!)

Here's Roland's message from a past Stroke TV show, "What Makes You Smile?"

> *"What you focus on, expands. Be joyful... It's not always easy, is it? Life has its ups and downs. Life has problems... Facing reality, to me, is too much of accepting what I don't want. I don't think*

PREFACE

God meant for that to happen. I think God meant, your wish is my command. You can expand in joy and can have all that you need because God has your back.

"Even if someone is limited in what they can do, we can still do things that brighten someone's day. We have a choice to either expand in joy or not. I feel like I am the happiest person I know. For me, that's the best I can be.

"We all have that choice. The more you choose to do it, that's what the Universe reflects and gives back to you. Now, I could be wrong about that, but I don't think so. I would challenge everyone to at least try it... You too can expand in joy. Most people would agree. Too often, we know this in our hearts, but we don't do it. We don't consistently expand in joy.

"I think I'm getting pretty good at it... Even if I'm being skeptical about one of my clients, I still feel inside that my goal is to guide them towards the better Self. It's going to be different for everyone. But if they choose to make life a little better, then my job is done."

To watch that program in its entirety, visit: http://bit.ly/StrokeTV1

I deeply regret that Roland suddenly passed from this earth on August 23, 2018. He had told me earlier that he was not afraid of dying. But I certainly didn't think he would be gone so quickly.

While I don't want to dwell on the sadness of Roland's passing, I do want to share the wondrous events that happened right before and after Roland's passing.

I learned about Roland's fourth stroke on Tuesday, August 21, through a text message from his wife, Barbara. I had a strong feeling he wasn't going to survive, but I didn't want to think negatively.

When Barbara told me that Roland was in intensive care and on a breathing tube, barely conscious, I felt compelled to do something. I

ROLAND'S STORY

wanted to believe that somehow, someway, he could recover. I figured if my prayer alone could be helpful in healing, perhaps a large group of prayers would have a bigger impact.

In less than 24 hours, thanks to help from several of Roland's buddies like Lowell Ann Fulsang, Aaron Avila and others, we gathered a number of people together for a *Get Well, Roland* online program. Friends appeared on the computer screen from across the world!

Everyone had thoughtful, loving comments to say to Roland. We all hoped Roland would hear our words eventually... or even through spirit. Shira Hunt later told me that she felt Roland's spirit with us during the program, and that he heard everything in spirit. I appreciated everyone's loving effort to send Roland healing energy, and was hoping for a miracle.

The next day, on August 23rd, 2018, at about 12:30 pm (CST), I received a text message from Barbara that Roland was gone. My heart seemed to stop.

"No!" I groaned, starting to cry. I didn't want to make a sound because I was substituting at the front desk of my husband's dental office. Heartbroken, tears streamed down my face. I hurried over to Joel to tell him the upsetting news.

"You need to leave," Joel said softly, gently escorting me out the door. I drove to my close friend Polly's home, just to have somewhere to go and cry. It felt so comforting to have her presence nearby. After a few minutes, I thought I'd call Joel to let him know how I was doing.

Since the internet reception wasn't working well inside Polly's home, I took my cell phone outside, ready to make the call. But Joel called me first! He wanted to check on me. As I held the phone in my right hand, out of the corner of my eye, I noticed something black, softly resting on my left wrist.

PREFACE

I turned my head to look more closely. Wow! It was a black and yellow-striped butterfly… sitting on my wrist!

Never in my life has anything like that ever happened. That butterfly just sat there for a few minutes. I was awestruck. Without a moment's hesitation, I KNEW it was a greeting… a sign from Roland's spirit. How amazing! Roland flew over to show me that his spirit is alive.

May this book give each of you a chance to experience Roland's fun, positive personality, and may it uplift you too. I'm forever thankful to Roland for shining his bright light into my life and so many others.

Feel free to share this memoir with your friends and family. Give it to those who need a boost of hope, encouragement, humor and positivity. Although Roland is no longer with us physically, his spirit lives on.

Roland's legacy continues through his story and his message: "EXPAND IN JOY!" I am forever grateful to have known his beautiful soul.

Each of us makes a difference in this world. Let us choose to follow Roland's example and make a conscious decision to live with joy.

– By Lynn B. Sanders, Founder/President of Difference Makers Media, LLC. Award-Winning Author of *Dancing With Tex: The Remarkable Friendship To Save The Whooping Cranes*, and *Social Justice: How You Can Make A Difference.*

PART I
In the Hospital

1

SPECIAL DELIVERY

Network television. Classic movies channel. Some of which I had been missing for years.

At home we didn't have cable, or even local stations. Just Netflix. So, this new array of options was something of a treat. Old Tarzan movies...cheesy romances... macabre mysteries... Laurel and Hardy black-n'-whites... Charlie Chaplin silent features... I got to catch up on stuff I'd never seen before although they'd been around for decades. I'd just never spent so much time as a channel changer. Didn't have the time... until now.

When regaining initial stability in the emergency room, it was a major plus to have basic TV... somewhat of an extravagance. Of course, it wasn't exactly a fair compensation for the paralysis of my right arm and leg. At first I actually had some of my foot, but in a few short days that small bit of control that allowed me to move my toes joined my other lost abilities such as walking, sitting up in bed, and using the toilet. My arm had a lot of what the therapists

ROLAND'S STORY

called "tone spasticity" - muscles, like my bicep, torquing my arm across my chest, with my hand knotted in a contorted fist that was reminiscent of another disease altogether. Otherwise, I couldn't really consciously do much with that limb either. Both right arm and leg, for the most part, were no longer mine to control.

A couple of days earlier I had experienced my third stroke. Waking up at six A.M. to go to the john, I couldn't get my back off the bed.

"C'mon, try again... gotta go... wake the bod up... done it a million times..."

Nope. It wasn't working. I intelligently worked it out in my defogging brain that there was a problem. Dawning reality brought with it the fact that I really had to go badly. As I struggled, I began to pee on myself. That was when I knew that I had to wake my wife.

Since this was not my first stroke I had a pretty good idea of what to expect. Barbara was in instant action, never one to panic, and always immediately practical. When things went wrong, it was always good to have her there. A 911 call... yes, emergency... address...

In a few short minutes, there were the double sirens. I knew a very efficient crew would be there in almost no time, with a series of questions I was becoming all too familiar with - "what's your name? ... do you know what day it is? ... how old are you? ... when did you first realize you had a problem? ... are you allergic to any medicines?" Then, a fast ride strapped in the miracle gurney that would adjust in height, load me into the ambulance with the help of one paramedic, and see me all the way to the emergency room bed.

Meanwhile as I waited, still getting to know my condition, I tried moving. I ended up on the floor, kind of leaning on my head. Fortunately, the gang did get there quickly, and soon I was on the express ride that could run red lights and ignore most traffic laws. They could even speed a little. It's amazing how fast a response there is

SPECIAL DELIVERY

in Orange County when your life is in medical danger. I wonder if the police are that fast? ... never mind.

During the wait Barbara had rushed in preparing things - I.D.; cell phone; getting dressed; and making sure that the front door was open and the household was awake; eliminating obstacles, and making sure that the emergency admission clerk wouldn't have any.

Somehow I was able to relax. It didn't occur to me that it just might be "my time to go." I was still alive, wasn't I? I still barely had the luxury of believing that it was for a good reason. I tried not to look out the side or rear windows as we were moving. Being prone to motion sickness, adding that to my issues wasn't a pleasant idea. I held my eyelids lightly shut and tried to breathe evenly and remain calm.

Before long the ambulance was pulling up to Saint Michael's Hospital. I was somewhat comforted in knowing from my previous trip for the same problem seven months ago that they had one of the most well-known stroke centers in Orange County. Inside of twenty minutes from the time I had awakened, I was being admitted into emergency.

The paramedics expertly manipulated my completely cooperative, but mostly unhelpful, hulk into a hospital bed. These beds must be expensive. They can raise, lower, sit you up, raise your knees, and even tip your whole body so that your head is a lower altitude than your feet. Shortly, I was to discover the value of having a powered machine bed with such a wide array of flexible attributes. Underneath this formidable collection of hydraulics were a set of wheels that, in a pinch, could effectively roll you over any minor debris that could clutter a hospital room floor.

The day was passing, and I was getting more and more tired. Mid-afternoon, I was startled to peer through the glass walls of the emergency and into the hallway, and see someone I knew.

ROLAND'S STORY

"Hey, I know that guy… we play racquetball together!" It was Reggie. He had recently come to Orange County from some state back east, and I had been the one to introduce myself, and invite him to play with our gang that met three times a week at LA Fitness.

The nurse pointed to him and said, "That man there? You know him?" I nodded. She walked out into the hall and summoned him in. "Reggie, this man says he knows you." Reggie looked through the glass at me and stared momentarily. Then his eyes widened and mouth dropped open, he hustled into the room to greet me.

"Roland! Hi! Man, what happened?"

I mumbled my explanation and told him about my stroke, and Reggie reciprocated, telling me that he was the admitting doctor for the emergency room. After some minutes, Reggie returned to his work. As he was leaving, he said to the nurse, "We're going to take extra special care of this guy – he's a friend of mine."

More questions for Barbara and me. No, sorry… I can't sign. Barbara handled it. Blah, blah, blah… Getting incredibly drowsy. Ah, well… I was in good hands.

2

THE LAUGH SPASM

In good hands.
If only I had arrived significantly sooner, like a few hours, instead of seven or eight. Under more timely circumstances, the doctors may have prescribed something referred to as, "tPA." Not a misspelling. Some genius decided that it was important to deemphasize the "t."

I had to look it up long after it was not a treatment option. It stands for, "Tissue Plasminogen Activator." So, why the small "t?" Beats me. Plasminogen. The name had a striking resemblance to something that bothered me... oh yeah, "carcinogen." But I have to wonder just how practical a drug might be from a doctor who spends that time contemplating how to abuse the English language in a nonsensical fashion, just because he has enough clout in his field to get everyone to agree.

It turned out that in order to be considered a candidate for the application of tPA, I would have had to have been in the emergency

ROLAND'S STORY

doctor's care within three hours. Labs and a CT scan would have taken some of that time. Scheduling those tests is harder than getting "tech support" from a foreign country, where there are too many employees getting paid too little per hour for the privilege of serving up solutions... but you still have to wait.

Several days later I was still curious, and in looking up tPA, I learned some shocking news. This drug that everyone was so excited about experimenting with for the purpose of my potential benefit, had some potentially horrific side effects as well.

The drug has the potential - not the ability, mind you - of breaking down blood clots that cause an inhibition of blood flow to the brain. The problem was that tPA could also cause, as one specialist puts it, "catastrophic bleeding to the brain." But they didn't mention that. My condition left me, for all intents and purposes, limp and lame. I wouldn't have been in the best condition to consider the pros and cons. Lawyers in a judicial arena may have declared me incompetent to represent myself.

After discussing it for a casual hour or two, the doctors determined that it was definitely too late for tPA to be effective. As I lay there too exhausted to maintain consciousness, I couldn't help but feel a bit of relief for not having had to make the call, nor to make Barbara deal with it. Revisiting the subject a day later, I was informed that I had no blood clot. The viscosity of my blood could be controlled via more docile compounds, more along the lines of aspirin. There would be more pills and injections to follow. But for now, everything was fed to me intravenously, dripping miserably and unsatisfyingly through a little tube.

They would not allow me to eat anything solid, nor even consume liquid, until I had passed the notorious "swallow test." But that wasn't going to happen until after I had spent a second night.

THE LAUGH SPASM

So, if I didn't have a blood clot, what did I have? A stroke is a clear sign that, for whatever reason, brain cells perished in your head. Those cells are connected to a series of neural pathways that allow the signals from your brain to reach all parts of your body. Apparently, the part of my brain that governed over my right arm and leg suffered the death of some brain cells.

I started speculating with my brain cells that were still alive. How many did I lose? Was it just a few brain cells? Hundreds or thousands? Millions? From what I knew of cells - which was limited, and probably left over from high school and Reader's Digest articles – I may have lost an enormous numerical quantity that took up an area the size of a pinhead. And why did they die? I knew that it was from lack of effective blood flow. But why the lack of blood?

I endured a series of tests, most of which required me to simply lie on a table or on my transport bed, remaining motionless for much longer than I probably remain still while I sleep, while a huge contraption moved about me, not requiring my ability to move, taking what I concluded from the preparation to be radioactive ray gun scans.

The technician was always quite clinical. "We'll have you outta here in just a little while..."

Oh, great. Then I get to travel down hospital corridors and elevators fighting my motion sickness again. Still too weak to sit up, by now probably due to lack of nutrition, I lay flat on my back while odd pictures of places and people no one knew streamed past; halls and doorways moving by too fast for me to read the signs; staff chatting with other staff members. In such a huge hospital with so many departments, it seemed as though an extraordinary number of staff were more than casual acquaintances.

"Hey! Haven't seen you for a few days." The response, "Oh yeah,

ROLAND'S STORY

well I took some vacation days." And back, "That's cool... and they moved me to ICU for the week, anyway." "Well I would have missed you regardless!" "Yeah. Well, call me this weekend?" "Will do!" "See ya!" "Bye!"

I wondered what they talked about in their off hours. It seemed that so many nurses, assistants, and technicians were long-standing employees. Maybe that was a good thing. One of the last things I wanted to hear about the hospital in which I was being treated for a critical condition was that there were a lot of newbies, trainees, and a high staff turnover rate.

Usually the last thing the tech said before a test started was along the lines of, "Okay now, for the next fifteen minutes you want to remain absolutely still! Try not to move!"

What exactly did they mean by that? I had to breathe, right? What if I had an itch? When someone tells you that you can't move for minutes at a time, the first thing you're sure of is that you have an itch. Aren't you scanning my skull? Can't I move my hands?

I managed to stay pretty motionless, other than the rise and fall of my chest from breathing, and ignored the two or three itchy places that I had not noticed until they said not to move. I guess it was good enough. The same issue was repeated in several tests with machines that worked me over, under, around, and through me: CT scan, MRI, EKG, EEG, ultrasound, and a few others. By the morning of third day, the doctors were going to be able to give me a snapshot of my situation. But for now, I had to rely on them doing their jobs.

It was late afternoon. Upon arriving back at my room, Barbara was there, sitting in a fairly comfortable chair that apparently could convert into a bed of sorts. If necessary, patient's family members were allowed to stay overnight. As close as we lived to the hospital I was determined not to allow her to do that. She was flipping through sheets of paper that obviously had everything to do with me occupying an emergency room bed.

"Hi. Baby! How're you feeling?" While I lay in bed getting more accustomed to my immobility, she had shifted into overdrive, making sure that the home front was running smoothly while we dealt with this new issue, and researching what we needed to do to best navigate my healthcare challenges.

"Okay, sweetie... I think I'm finally done testing for now." I wasn't a complainer, and always tried to look at things positively – and I was positive that complaining wasn't going to improve my experience, or speed up my recovery. Everything that had been scheduled was done. Although nothing required strenuous effort from me, I wasn't getting any rest, either. Shortly after one test finished, I was on my way to the next. It seemed like I was wheeled to the far reaches of the hospital for each test, with none of them in the same section. Was it just bad planning? Or did these tests represent such diverse aspects of treatment and healthcare that the test equipment would be found in different wings and floors of the hospital?

"How're you? Hangin' in there?" I queried, knowing that she was working extra hard as a side effect of my hospitalization.

"I'm fine." She responded cheerily, even though I knew she was sacrificing sleep, and being very busy trying to work time slots into her schedule so she could hurry down to the hospital and join me in my holding pattern of life. "My manager let me off early to take care of a few things. I went to the store for groceries, put gas in my car, and went and paid the phone bill."

"Oh, thanks. I appreciate that." The phone bill was my responsibility. I was glad that she had remembered for me. Barbara and I, and all of our kids, were on that cell phone plan. It occurred to me that I'd have to contact everyone soon – the kids, Mom, my sisters, some close friends and some active clients. I was right handed, and I couldn't wrap my brain around how I was going to do my job, designing websites and working with critical graphics projects, without it. Well, I wouldn't concern myself tonight.

"Did they give you the swallow test? I was hoping to have dinner with you." I just shook my head no. It was one of the few things that I could still move.

"Not yet," I said with a creeping desolation, wondering how a second whole day could pass with no attention to this detail. "You're going to have to eat without me." She looked at me in dismay. She knew that I was getting seriously hungry.

Just then the nurse walked in. "Time to take your vitals!" It was Alison, the day nurse, and she'd been caring for me all day. So far, I think that this was the fourth or fifth time since daybreak that she performed this task. Even during the night, the night nurse had awakened me repeatedly to do the same. I judged that all emergency room patients got their vital signs checked every two hours. Alison was nice, and genuinely cared for people. She was good medicine. She rolled a rather large contraption over to me that looked like a combination equipment rack and toiletry dispenser. "How are you doing? Can I get you anything?"

"A filet, medium rare, with some steamed vegies and wild rice." Barbara and I had to grin. So did Alison. She took the joke lightly, smiling in her constantly pleasant way, and said, "Sadly, that request will have to wait just a little longer."

"I'll be patient," I said, and the pun didn't escape Alison, whose smile broke into laughter. Barbara and I laughed too.

I noticed something strange with my body. I reacted to the simple pun with much more of a response than was due. I really thought that I was clever. But not only that, I laughed as though the patient quip

THE LAUGH SPASM

had much more humor invested in it than a simple pun. I'd have to calm down. I was raising my blood pressure, and Alison was about to take my vitals.

Okay... deep breath... relax...

Alison wrapped the arm "collar" around the bicep of my left arm, and while the compression pump filled it with air, and it tightened around my arm until it was decidedly uncomfortable, she also took the utility rack's thermometer, which was connected to a different gadget, and placed it, sterile plastic coated, into my mouth. Inside of 30 seconds she was done with both checks, and removing the thermometer and collar, and reporting her finds.

"One-eighty over one-twenty... pulse, 62... and temperature, ninety-six-point-five." It alarmed me. I knew that normal blood pressure was one-twenty over eighty. Also, wasn't my temperature supposed to be ninety-eight-point-six? I had always thought that plus two degrees was a mild temperature, and minus two and you'd better check the pulse.

"Wow, that's high. And my temperature is low..." I said with obvious alarm in my voice.

"It's okay. The doctor wants it a little high. Since your stroke, he wants to make sure you're getting enough blood to all parts of your brain." Alison explained. She could see my concern for high blood pressure, but didn't seem bothered by the fact that my blood was on the cool side. Well, if Alison wasn't concerned, I wasn't either. "It's alright for now," she said.

At least I was in the right place if the doctor decided to do something about it. Alison logged the readings and rolled the rack away. "Man, that's high," I said to Barbara. "But I guess we don't have to worry about it for now."

She nodded in agreement. "I'm sure you're okay. We can watch a movie or something."

ROLAND'S STORY

"Sounds good." I had scoped out all the stations repeatedly... all twelve of them. At least there was the Turner Movie Classics channel – a continuous flow of old movies worthy of a well-known critic's personal commentary before and after each one. Little did I know that the master of ceremonies of that station was going to start feeling like my best buddy. The communication was, of course, one way. But he was so serene and sure of himself that he was like the trusted uncle sharing words of wisdom. In between his periodic dissertations on the movies, there were commercials telling of upcoming shows, preparing the viewer for the pleasures that awaited, and building anticipation.

I had to admit, several shows sounded good, although some missed striking any nerve whatsoever. Regarding those that seemed less than interesting, I got used to hoping for a surprise, and sometimes the movies did indeed surprise me. Other movies caused me to wonder about the authority of my grey-haired adopted uncle on the screen, and his incentive to endorse such pitiful plots and productions. I guess there were some aspects of movie appreciation about which I had no clue. Yet on occasion, there was a film that promised to be quite entertaining.

One that had captured my attention was "Ben Hur," a truly great classic that I had seen, but it had been years, or perhaps decades. I had mentally recorded for future reference that it was on that evening.

"Ben Hur is on Turner Classics at seven," I announced to Barbara.

"Oh, I've heard of that," she said. "I don't think I've seen it."

"It has one of the most famous action scenes in movie history – the chariot race. Charlton Heston is actually driving a chariot. It was a seriously dangerous production and one driver was actually seriously injured, his actual blood being kept in the scene." I was well informed from the repeated ads that I had watched, and the

THE LAUGH SPASM

announcer's passionate description of the historic saga. I was actually looking forward to this one.

We decided to watch it, and proceeded to pass the time channel changing and watching various programs. It was after six-thirty, when my mind took me back to a childhood moment, immortalized by the telling of a one-liner joke.

It was a testimony to my memory, and to the movie, Ben Hur, because, without the movie, I surely would not have recognized the significance of the joke. Now, I am in no way, shape, or form a racist, and have been known to poke fun at the fact that I am of Japanese heritage, along with all its cultural significance and trademarks that make comic icons of slanted eyes, and broken English that replaces "Ls" with "Rs." So it was with a sense of comedic license that I had fun with all kinds of ethnic humor, like the one I was about to tell Barbara, and learned when I was a mere ten years old.

The memory of the joke had me instantaneously smiling. I think I learned it from the same guy who asked me, "What's green, has sideburns, and plays the guitar?" And the answer is, "Elvis Parsley!" I felt a strange impulse growing in my stomach as I prepared the delivery of one of the oldest jokes I knew. Barbara watched me with interest as she could see I was having some fun.

"I have a joke..." I announced. And the growing sensation in my midsection was now infiltrating more of me. I started to hurry. "It's kind of a stupid joke, but it's funny..."

"What's brown and rides a chariot?" I could feel the pressure building incredibly.

"I don't know. What?" She answered dutifully.

I started to throw the punch line. "B......." And that's as far as I got.

Suddenly the funny bone of my body was smacked by the humor-hammer, and I caved in on myself, all of my muscles clenching in unison so that I lost all composure and control, and wheezed all of the air out of my lungs. After the longest exhale of my life, I managed to capture a breath. But it was no use. I was gripped in the giant hand of the muse-monster, and he wasn't letting go. I couldn't get a word out. As I tried to regain some command over myself, another wave caught me and I was once again rendered helpless.

Barbara, still waiting for the joke's punch line, was nonetheless moved by my infectious state, which was, no doubt, quite comical. She started to laugh. Tears were streaming down my face, and the fits of exhales were still abusing my body. I could see that Barbara was dabbing at her own eyes. Several times the laughter subsided, and I considered trying to complete what I had started several minutes ago. Anyone who walked in on us would have taken one look and sworn that I had successfully finished the telling of a funny joke.

All of fifteen minutes had passed before I could give Barbara an audible and sober two words, "Ben Hernandez." The image of a short, stocky Hispanic male, being pulled by four horses and riding a chariot while trying to keep his sombrero on his head was quite comical. But I guess I was laughed out.

"I have to admit, that's pretty funny."

I was sorry for the utter destruction of the joke, but glad it was appreciated. I took a break from comic relief to revive myself: no speech therapist and no dinner. Barbara suffered through with me, declaring that she wasn't hungry. I knew she was just being supportive. That's my Barbara.

It was almost seven o'clock. In came Alison rolling the rig. "It's that time again."

Oh, great. I bet my blood pressure was up. That cracked me up, too, although it was not as crippling as it had been twenty minutes

THE LAUGH SPASM

ago. I consciously calmed myself, taking as deep a breath as I was capable.

Alison performed the tasks, and determined that I was a bit high on all my stats. "Hmmm... we'll have to keep a good watch on you. I may check you again in a few minutes. By the way, it's almost time for shift changes, so I'll be leaving soon."

Barbara had made it through most of Ben Hur in spirit only, with consciousness adrift, for the most part. I finally shut off the TV and suggested that she call it a night. She gathered her things, gave me a kiss, and ambled out into the hall. I heard her talking with the night nurse, and couldn't make out what they were saying.

It had been a long day of laying there. I turned the TV back on to finish watching Ben Hur. If I made it, I have no memory of it. I was to become well acquainted with many new experiences in the coming days.

There was learning to eat left-handed; opening packets of sugar-free jelly, fake butter, and creamer one-handed; and figuring out how to use a urinal. Initially, there was a lot of frustration trying to access things and do stuff that had once been easy. I adjusted my expectations accordingly, and developed a greater degree of patience than I'd ever had.

It was a radically different ball game, but I wasn't agreeable with the concept of striking out. Batter up!

3

THE LAUGH SPASM REVISITED

I would be in the emergency section of the hospital a couple more days. Every so often Reggie would stream in and spend a few minutes. I felt like I had some clout by knowing the Chief of Admissions. It made me feel better to know he was there.

Barbara happened to have the next day off. Her general manager was probably trying to help. She very seldom had Mondays off. After rising to meet the day from a much needed night's sleep, she made her son, Kyle, a quick breakfast, worked her way through more medical paperwork, and headed for the hospital.

Breakfast was once again a missed opportunity, and I was praying that the nurse would have mercy and give me a cup of coffee. She arrived on the heels of Dr Nori, the neurologist.

"Hi, Mr. Takaoka. How are you feeling?" It sounded much too formal for a doctor bringing pleasant news.

"I'm okay. Dr. Nori, this is my wife, Barbara." He took her hand

THE LAUGH SPASM REVISITED

lightly, and they exchanged greetings. I could imagine him heading immediately over to the dispenser on the wall which was probably like the one in every emergency room, rationing out the right amount of hand sanitizer to kill any germs exclusive to that room.

"We have had a chance to thoroughly scrutinize your x-rays and scans, and determined you definitely had a stroke," the neurologist was addressing the subject of his visit and reason for my temporary residence.

I began questioning before he had a chance to explain further, "Okay... did I have a blood clot?"

"No." he said.

"Plaque from cholesterol?"

"Well, a little... not much."

"A hemorrhage?" I asked.

"No, no bleeding."

"Well, then what?" I was perplexed.

The doctor continued to try and explain. "You have, near your brain stem, on the left side, sort of behind the ear, a tiny blood vessel that is constricted, and your blood is thicker than it should be, and your blood pressure is high. So your system is stressed, and trying desperately to get blood to that portion of the brain... and it is failing to do so."

"That's it?" I said.

He replied, "Yes, that's it. And you are type 2 diabetic, so that doesn't help. You eat carbohydrates, sugar, and it thickens your blood even more. All carbohydrates turn to sugar when metabolized."

I hadn't had it explained like that. I had been warned that carbs turned to sugar, but not that sugar thickens the blood. Thinking about it, I realized that it made sense – sugar thickens everything else, doesn't it? A no-brainer. Uh... maybe a bad choice of words.

ROLAND'S STORY

"So, what now?" I asked.

"You mean, what can we do now? Not much. When brain cells die, they don't come back. Sets of conglomerate cells are responsible for various parts of your body. The more cells that die, the more extensive, and the more permanent, the damage."

I was not enjoying this speech. I looked at Barbara, and she raised her eyebrows at me as if to say, "... and now for the good news?" I turned my attention back to Dr. Nori, and said, "But I, myself, have recovered from two minor strokes. I was back to playing racquetball full speed, three hours, three times a week!"

I began to worry, just a little. Prior to this event, some physicians had warned me that another stroke could occur, and it could be worse. I could have more, and they could take a greater toll on my body. As well as losing the use of arms and legs, I could lose my ability to speak. As it was, I was having some trouble with speaking clearly. It was an effort to move my tongue, and formulate the words that had always flowed so eloquently and effortlessly, prior to this stroke.

My tongue... that started me thinking about my swallow test again. The speech therapist was due anytime now, and I wanted to hear that I was cleared for solid foods. I still had been given nothing but a couple of sips water for more than two days.

Dr. Nori wrapped up his presentation.

"I am sorry to tell it this way, but we have no way of knowing for sure if you will partially or fully recover. There is just no way of knowing. The therapists will be working with you, and we'll see. Sometimes it takes weeks or months... even years. Quite often most of the recovery occurs within the first three months. And after one year, usually anything that's going to come back is back. It could be a lifelong process. And, there could be no recovery at all. For now,

THE LAUGH SPASM REVISITED

the best thing to do is get lots of rest, and let your body recover. It has suffered an acute trauma. I'll check in tomorrow. Later today they'll be moving you out of emergency, and into your own room."

The doctor was not very well-practiced at inspirational talks. I was noticing a similarity with a few other doctors as well.

It was a bit disturbing that, although I was known for being an optimist, there were some solid obstacles for me to deal with that were dampening my cheerfulness, and this time I literally couldn't walk away from the facts. I lay on my back, nearly split down the middle, with my left side timing out and my right side MIA. In general, I felt too weak to care about anything but getting some sleep, and "wake me if you'll feed me."

As the doctor headed for the door, sure enough, he passed by the sanitizer dispenser, got a measured dose of 'kills-all," and went out without looking back. After the soothsayer of doom and gloom went away, I couldn't muster the strength to wonder.

Barbara saw that I was fading after absorbing the news, and suggested that I not be concerned with her presence, and get some rest as the doctor had ordered. So I was dozing when the speech therapist finally arrived, carrying a hospital tray with a dish topped with a stainless steel cover that looked like a prop from the classic sci-fi, "Earth VS. The Flying Saucers." I had just watched it a day ago.

Since I was lame and sleepy, I was pretty much in neutral as Barbara entered the room. Not my Barbara, but Barbara the speech therapist. I took as deep a breath as I could, and realized that I encountered some difficulty trying to inhale. My Barbara rose from her chair and walked over to welcome the therapist on my behalf, like it might improve the score she gave me when she administered the swallow test. But I knew that Barbara was just being herself, polite and cordial, and expecting positive results was a foregone conclusion. She couldn't imagine me not passing, and would not entertain the possibility of failure.

The therapist turned to me. "Hello, Mr. Ta... Taka.... Tako-aka?" She said with some difficulty, getting the middle two vowels of my name backwards. In her defense, I think that I have heard hundreds of variations of my last name, which was amazing. I mean, can you actually even randomly scramble seven letters that many ways? I was considering doing a quick mental calculation, but decided that it was seriously too much of a project for what it was worth. Well, there had to be dozens, at least. People saw all the "a's" and "k's," and anticipated some exotic pronunciation, when it was really quite simple. So, I was instantaneously forgiving.

Then, before I could venture forth with a response, I had a thought that caused me to have a laugh seizure again, a repeat of the night before. Here was a "speech therapist" having a problem pronouncing my name. It was just humorous enough to cause me to chuckle. But somehow a chuckle wasn't an event that I was equipped to accommodate. I expelled the common short exhale that usually accompanied the, "Ha!" in normal circumstances. The short exhale was extended, and followed by a full body cramp that focused on my gut and chest, threatening to hold me in smother mode until I had passed out from lack of air. This obviously was a new and ongoing condition of the last couple of days.

All I could do was grin fiendishly and wait for the cramp to subside. My face was inhabited with a kind of comical expression of possession that called for an exorcism. Visions of Batman's bane, "The Joker," came to mind. That was funny too, but I couldn't explain that either. I realized that tears were trickling down both of my cheeks. This condition had to be a result of having the stroke. Apparently, it wasn't just my arm and leg having issues.

THE LAUGH SPASM REVISITED

I managed to get a partial breath. Then, with my mind still on the subject of my seizure, I immediately cramped up again with a hard body spasm that should have been a simple laugh, but was a serious muscle issue threatening my weakened system. As the spasm subsided, I tried to concentrate on calming down, took a couple of quick breaths, and tried to wipe away some of the tears. I told myself that if I wasn't careful I'd put too much pressure on my head and burst a blood vessel... and then, that too found my ticklish spot, and I ungraciously seized up again.

I waved playfully at Barbara and Barbara, and soundlessly mouthed the words, "I'm sorry..." The therapist actually grinned at me pleasantly, accommodating my spasm, allowing me to recover myself, such as I was. My wife struggled a bit, remembering the night before, and managed to keep her contribution to a light chuckle. "Heh, heh, heh...."

"I'm so sorry... I couldn't help myself," I said with a sort of drawl that wasn't there a couple of days ago, and made note of numbness in my mouth on the right side. It kind of felt as if pinching fingers were holding onto my lips and cheek, retarding their normal functionality. Also, the tension of the cramping seemed to cause my voice to rise in pitch. I was speaking like a little girl.

"It's okay," she said. "Are you alright?" Her concern was genuine, and she seemed a little perplexed, like she hadn't witnessed that kind of symptom in a patient before. She had set the tray down along with a manila folder. I took my time recomposing myself, and hand-signed, pinching my thumb and forefinger, with my other three fingers spread - "A – Okay!"

"I'm fine now. And the name is Ta-ka-o-ka, and almost everybody has their own way of pronouncing it. I'll answer to just about anything. Just call me Roland, please."

ROLAND'S STORY

She smiled more widely, and seemed a bit relieved. I thought about explaining the joke that had originally started me on my disabling seizure. I felt a light cramping begin, and decided it wasn't likely that I would survive another round, so I conscientiously returned my focus to the subject at hand. "So, you're here for my swallow test?" At this point, I was seriously concerned as to how I was going to do. Before that moment, I had not considered the possibility of failure.

"Yes. I asked them to order a lunch plate a little early since we missed breakfast, and as I understand it, you haven't eaten yet since you were admitted." It was a statement, but she raised her tone a bit, almost like she was asking a question. She reached for the tray which she had set on the rolling table designed to extend over bodies in hospital beds. I decided I liked her. Removing the flying saucer and setting it aside, she then picked up the plastic knife and fork.

"That's right, and I'm really looking forward to this. I suspect I'll be allowed to eat the whole lunch, not just the test bites?" I was still feeling the effects of humor tracking through my thoughts, and I was in a pretty good mood. My Barbara was still grinning.

"Oh, of course. But let's see how you do first, before we come to any conclusions." I was going to get the full introductory lecture. "First we'll give you a small piece of this chicken and have you chew and swallow it. Then I'll be able to tell if you're having any issues with eating solids. Very commonly, with stroke victims, one side of the face or the other is affected, and if your swallowing muscles are impaired you could possibly choke on your food."

"Okay, I am so ready..." Finally, the problem of satisfying my empty belly was about to be vanquished. Or, was it...

The tester rolled the tray closer to me, not yet positioning it as if the plate of food belonged to me. She kept it alongside the bed, but not in between herself and me. The food was actually steaming, and

THE LAUGH SPASM REVISITED

having been in the hospital before, I knew that they couldn't do too much damage to a chicken filet.

Holding the chicken in place with the fork, she went to work carving a bite that was no bigger than a half inch cube. Then stabbing the cube with the fork, she offered it to me. I leaned toward the bite, extending with my neck. Taking the petite bite and scraping it off the fork, I began chewing the chicken on the right side of my mouth, being careful not to bite my lip, which was a tiny bit numb, but not enough to be an issue. This was going to be a piece of cake.

I chewed quickly and swallowed, thinking that all she wanted was proof that I could swallow solid food. As I was finishing the chicken remnants she said, "Okay, open your mouth."

Still chewing the remaining shreds, I thought that this was a little premature, seeing as though I was still finishing up. But I complied. Opening my mouth, I showed her that I had successfully eaten most of the chicken that she had carefully diced for me. But the look on her face was not one of celebration.

She hesitated... speaking slowly. "Uh, there's a little bit of chicken still there on the right side..."

"Sure," I stated as if confirming that she hadn't given me a fair chance to finish.

"Let's try that again," she said, hastily cutting another small cube of chicken.

Offering the chicken again, I repeated my performance, chewing on the right side again. How was she supposed to know that the space between my teeth on the left side of my mouth was a notorious catch-all for sinewy foods like chicken and beef, and I was conscientiously avoiding the trap?

The "speech-therapist-turned-servant" waited just long enough for me to chew most of the piece of chicken into a digestible mass, and said, "Open... let's see." She peered into my mouth, and announced, "See! There's still a little bit of chicken on the right side." I could tell my wife was smiling, even though her hand hid her mouth.

I was startled by the way she announced her discovery, as if something of shocking significance had revealed itself. Incredulous, I tried to explain to her what seemed so obvious to me. "That's because I'm chewing on the right side!" My Barbara started to giggle openly.

"What?" She shook her head lightly, and couldn't comprehend the issue.

"Look," I said, "give me another piece of chicken." She diligently assumed her job as food server, and soon a third chicken cube was headed my way. "Okay, now watch..."

I took the chicken as I had the first two times, except I maneuvered the chicken toward the left side to challenge the food trap, chewed and swallowed, knowing I was going to need a toothpick soon, and timing it appropriately to be fair, I exposed the contents left in my mouth.

The therapist looked truly baffled. Perhaps she was speechless. In a state of bewilderment, she slowly described her findings, "Now... there's some... chicken... on... the... LEFT side..."

"That's because I'm chewing on the LEFT SIDE!" I said with appropriate emphasis.

The puzzle was untangling, and her bewildered look transformed into one of understanding and wide-eyed surprise. "OHHHH... I see!" she exclaimed. "Well, chew on both sides!"

"Well, give me a bigger piece of chicken!" I demanded. And suddenly, we were all laughing hilariously... except me... technically, I was having a laughing seizure, trying to catch my breath, tears and all, while trying not to choke on chicken shreds. Surviving this, I

THE LAUGH SPASM REVISITED

was cleared for take-off, and soon well on my way, flying through my early lunch.

Later that day, they announced that I had been awarded my very own room in the stroke wing of the hospital. I was going to get to know all different nurses, day and night staff, and the assistants, called CNA's. And they were going to get to know me, too... some, better than others.

By late afternoon, they told me I'd be relocated before my dinner came. At that point, that was all I wanted to know.

4

MENU AND OTHER CONDITIONS

Finally... FOOD!
Since the chicken plate had been a special order, the kitchen crew and servers weren't keeping an accurate account of what was delivered to my room.

At noon, the early lunch was followed by the normal lunch, and I was handed a second meal. Since I hadn't actually placed the order, I received the default selection - a deli plate – which meant an unassembled sandwich with cold cuts, sliced cheese, and crackers on a large leaf of iceberg lettuce, and no bread. Well, it did offer the crackers on the side. It would have been fairly acceptable under the circumstances if it had come with a couple packets of mayo and mustard. Fortunately, the nurse's station stored some condiments, which normally included these, but they were out of the traditional sandwich dressings. I settled for a packet of ranch salad dressing.

Just the mere fact that I had food to eat was a revelation. Not to

MENU AND OTHER CONDITIONS

mention that I could drink as much water as I pleased, and had the options of some types of juices, non-fat milk, and decaf coffee.

Taking my time and treating "the second coming of lunch" like a religious ceremony, I carefully chewed and swallowed every bite. These privileges were not without their issues, I was soon to find. I continuously discovered more problems related to food and drink consumption that I had not figured into the equation. However, there was one aspect that I was surprised and happy to discover. For each and every meal, we had multiple choices.

The afternoon passed onward with the normal routines, and before I was actually hungry again, here came dinner. I thoroughly enjoyed the overcooked green beans and the scoop of mashed potatoes with brown gravy, and some slices of turkey breast.

As I got near the end of the meal though, I was considering the fact that they also refer to green beans as "string beans," possibly because they appear long and stringy, or maybe because when cooked in a certain way, a way that the "Saint Michael's Master Chefs" apparently had perfected, the beans were indeed like string... nay, more like twine.

I went from chewing and swallowing partial mouthfuls, to spitting balls of green sinew back on the plate, to refusing entrance past my lips and teeth altogether. The last tactic proved to be the most acceptable, and became the modus operandi for green beans – rather, string beans - and for various reasons, this also became standard consumption protocol for an assortment of other hospital vegies that made the ban list.

Overall, the meals were fairly acceptable. I had heard repeatedly about how Saint Michael's Hospital was well-known for "better than average" fair. As time went on, I wondered who the critics could have been, who had the occasion to try the food from more than

ROLAND'S STORY

one facility in order to make the comparison. I was having some trouble imagining enough people in situations involving multiple locations that they could take a poll and get a consensus.

Nobody went to hospitals just to sample the menu. Yet, I was taken back in time when my Dad used to take me to the Fresno Community Hospital to have the biggest one dollar burger in town. Well, that was an exception. I was referred to as "the hamburger kid," and my Dad was happy to support the title. Hence, that was our reason for eating in the cafe of a healthcare facility when neither of us were physically unfit.

Of course, I'm still describing a hospital cafeteria that was being patronized by people whose presence was not determined by the need of the facility's professional services. Inevitably, I was later to become the self-appointed authority regarding healthcare institutional grub, proving that there were indeed situations in which healthcare facility patrons could be qualified to speak on the subject, and was my own best example of how someone could have first-hand experience.

In the meantime I was still building my credibility as a taste tester at the place in which I resided... and it truly started to feel like my residence. That meant I had to keep an open mind regarding dishes I had not yet tried if I was to find the most acceptable meals. I was to discover a wide variety of choices that were fairly diverse.

For instance, for breakfast there were eggs, of course, and an occasional piece of sausage or bacon. That is, until they realized that, because of my stroke, I was on the diet that called for low sodium. Then the sausage and bacon were to disappear indefinitely from my diet. However, this still left me with French toast and waffles, which lost some of their highlight when they replaced my syrup with something sugar free. But I had to respect that. They

MENU AND OTHER CONDITIONS

were accented by some small mini-tubs of something they casually referred to as butter, yet was another substitute for the real thing.

Lunch and dinner were remarkably similar. Seldom was lunch like a traditional lunch meal, such as a sandwich. However, they managed to work sandwiches into the dinner selections as well as lunch. There was an abundance of baked and grilled salmon, for which I was initially quite pleased, and ordered it whenever I could. By the third week salmon had amazingly achieved official status on the ban list, with a special note that it should be a punishable crime for any chef anywhere to ruin that much perfectly good fish. What should have been a tasty, flakey filet of fish was a consistent culinary catastrophe. Yes, a jail sentence seemed appropriate.

Selecting meals became both a recreation and a challenge. A pleasant lady by the name of Maria came once a day with a form and a pencil to fill out my choices for tomorrow's three meals. Over time, she made me aware of the weekly standards, and also the various options that they did not openly advertise. Maria learned my preferences and my needs, such as extra fake butter for my French toast, a packet of sugar substitute with my oatmeal, and "Paul Newman's Own Ranch Dressing Lite" with my salads. She had quite a good memory, and was truly a pleasant person. I always had a smile for her, and she had one for me too.

My new day nurse was named Deana. She spoke with a linguistic affect that had me baffled as to whether it was an accent from some eastern state or a speech defect. Yet, I could tell that she was a warm humanitarian, and she took good care of me.

I was starting to recognize the symptoms of hospitalization. My personal state was not the same as every stroke victim. Victim – that word had a strange effect on me. By definition, I was powerless to do anything to prevent the stroke. That left me with this creepy feeling

ROLAND'S STORY

that told me there was a demon in the dark somewhere. If and when he wanted to, he could silently strike out again, and gently lay me closer to a completely helpless condition. I shuddered at the idea of waking up from sleep again with more physical abilities taken away, and having no say as to whether I would ever walk again. I felt a real coldness for the first time since my trip to emergency.

When I first arrived, I still had a little wiggle to my right foot. Now, the ability to do even that much was gone. When I did a thorough self-examination, there were several things to note. For instance, even though I couldn't move my right arm or leg, I could still feel with both, and sense heat and cold, and even a feather's touch. That sensory ability included tickles, itches, and pain.

I realized that although I was left with the sense of touch, without any area of my body being so numb as to eliminate feeling, I was split sort of down the middle of my body in the ability to command movement. The line of demarcation was rather jagged as opposed to a perfect split down my center. An example being that I had normal feeling and movement in most of my face, except the corner of my mouth, and my cheek back to my ear. People could barely notice a weakness in my smile. The rest of my skull felt normal. But although my smile was fairly well-balanced visually, I still had issues drinking liquids without drooling, and winking my right eye.

As I became more aware of the selectiveness of my stroke-affected areas, I was thankful it had elected not to follow a perfect line, and shut down everything on the right half of my body indiscriminately. Whatever deciding force had opted to leave my vital organs functioning well enough to sustain me, I had to feel grateful. After all, the right half of me included one of my lungs, a kidney, most of my liver, and all of my gall bladder, not to mention my appendix, although I doubted that this last factoid mattered. At least all my

MENU AND OTHER CONDITIONS

vital organs seemed to be doing their jobs, and the doctors didn't seem concerned.

However, in the process of scrutinizing my physical state, I came to realize that, among other things, I had a breathing problem. I could not easily take a deep breath. I felt like a very large weight was sitting on my chest. Consequently, my shallow breathing wasn't feeding me oxygen consistently.

I developed two conditions that nurse Deana explained were more than likely due to the stroke. The first was that I now yawned frequently, sometimes every few minutes, and I didn't have to be particularly sleepy or tired. The second was that I often got the hiccups, sometimes a few in a row, and sometimes for several minutes at a time. I felt as though I were yawning and hiccupping all day. It became quite annoying. I never really got used to these two abnormal ailments, and they were impossible to ignore.

Itching had become a real hassle. It was compounded by the fact that I couldn't maneuver my body easily, and was constantly on my back. There were places on my body that I couldn't reach. This bothersome issue was magnified by some side elements. Wrinkles were the common culprit. Wrinkles came from my hospital gown, my bed sheet, the mattress, and another hospital hazard that I came to know quite intimately, a type of pillow, referred to as a "chuck."

Chucks serve a dual purpose, I came to realize. When I first got to the hospital they placed one approximately under my butt. However, in doing so, the chucks were positioned strategically for adjusting bodies in bed. I realized this on my first day when I was gradually sliding to the foot of the bed, and asked for help repositioning myself.

Nurse Deana answered the call for help, along with a sturdy looking man in his thirties named Martin. They knew exactly what to do. I guess I wasn't the first patient to raise this flag. They stood

ROLAND'S STORY

at attention on either side of the bed, and I didn't initially notice they were perfectly positioned relative to the chucks. I wondered if, because it was just one, it should technically be called, "chuck."

I could tell Deana was attending to some bed controls that were exclusive to staff, being on the outside of the raised bedrail. She touched a button, and oddly, not only did the control level the bed, but it raised my feet and dropped my head at the same time. The effect was that I felt like I was being tipped upside down, and gravity added pressure to my brain. It was dizzying.

"Oh, just get it done," I thought silently. I noticed that both Deana and Martin now had two-handed grips on "the chucks"... or "the chuck"... or maybe just "chuck." Deana asked me to hold my head up, which amplified my increasing sensation of nausea. Positioned and ready for my slide to begin, head raised as requested, they counted, "one... two... three!" in unison, and suddenly I felt my body floating towards the top of the bed. "Again!" Deana said, and they repeated the levitated slide.

They released their hold on chuck, and Deana, a hand on the bed control again, leveled my body. "How's that?" she asked. Even as I answered, I had nearly completely recovered from the momentary nausea.

"That's great," I said. "I'm not all cramped any more. Thanks a lot."

She responded in her odd little vocal style, "No worries, Mr. Takaoka. Whenever you need something you just call me." She sounded so sincere and genuinely dedicated that I was warmed by her statement. I also thought it was a bit odd the way she put it. A full service hospital? Anyway, her words were assuring, and I was much more comfortable.

"There is one thing," I added, as she headed for the door.

"What's that, honey?" It was an odd response, coming from my medical caretaker in this clinical atmosphere. I decided that it was borderline inappropriate. Well, she was just a nurse with a warm heart.

"Because I can't turn over easily, and can't reach my back, I have several itchy spots and they are driving me nuts!"

She headed for a tall cabinet straight away, and said as she traveled, "Oh…. I've got just the thing to cure that. We'll turn you onto your side for a bit, and I'll take care of it."

My imagination took control of my mental imagery, and visions of chains and whips invaded my consciousness. I wondered what ominous implement lay hidden behind the double doors, reserved for those poor souls who complained about itching. Deana opened the cabinet and reached inside, taking a medium hand towel from a shelf.

"These things work great for this. Let's roll you onto your side." She gently supported my upper and lower back with a hand each and helped me onto my right side. Then she exposed my back quite effectively by untying and parting the hospital robe. She began rubbing my back with the rolled up terry cloth hand towel, and the relief was amazing. Deana methodically and with great skill covered my back with the itch-killing strokes.

"Oh, my God!" I moaned, and utterly submitted myself to her treatment. "Oooh… I can't believe that."

Deana continued to work. "See… the best back scratcher!" I had to admit that, after that moment, I was totally sold on terry cloth back scratching. With my direction, she was able to locate three or four particularly needy areas.

From my moans, I half expected any passing hospital personnel to poke a head into the room from curiosity. The sounds did seem somewhat out of context for a patient's room.

"Yeah, I can tell why you're itchy from the creases in your skin.

ROLAND'S STORY

It's because of your gown and, uh... what's this from?" Her question had me puzzled. "Your gown didn't cause this. Ah... well, it's gotta be from the chucks." Across the middle of my back was a heavier array of crease marks in my skin. "It's pretty bad right across here." She rubbed over the heavier red marks left across my back from the chucks.

So, I guess whether it was one, or more, it was "chucks."

"These chucks are pretty handy." Deana bragged. "They're disposable, but they're really strong and can carry a lot of weight. Makes it so easy to move someone who's even much bigger than you. And also, they're waterproof. "

"Waterproof?" I asked.

… Which brings us back to the subject of chucks' dual purpose...

5

AN INTRO TO THERAPY

"Yes, waterproof." Deana was finishing explaining the values of chucks. "We use them with patients who can't make it easily to the bathroom, just in case we need to use urinals and bedpans." This seemed to remind Deana of something.

"As a matter of fact, did you have a bowel movement today?" It was a fair question. At the time I wasn't too concerned, because they hadn't been feeding me until the day before.

I answered, "No, but after all I've been eating it's bound to happen anytime now."

"Okay, well keep me posted, because it's important." She said. "Constipation is a common problem after strokes. Your system slows down, and you're not walking or exercising. So if there's a problem there are things we can do." She raised her eyebrows as if to emphasize the obvious.

"You mean like colase?" I had heard of pregnant moms having

to use such a thing, since constipation was apparently a common problem with pregnancy.

"Yeah, we have that, and I should probably give you one now just in case." Deana was quite proactive on my behalf. "Just a moment, and I'll add it to your meds list. I'll have a gelcap for you before you crash tonight. " She finished entering data in the computer, made some notes on my charts, and as she was leaving said, "Remember, I'm here for ya. Anything you need, let me know."

Deana seemed so congenial and pleasant. Still, I was feeling slightly uneasy, and I wasn't sure why. The thought of her looking forward to lovingly assisting me with my bedpan was intimidating. My fluent imagination took the whole vision to the next level, for I knew that if the colase didn't work, the next thing would be a suppository. I wished that she was a little more clinical and detached. That would have set my thoughts at ease. "Roland, you ditz... you're delusional! This is a hospital!"

I let it go. However, now I was thinking about a new challenge. Bed pans. In order to use the toilet I would have to be able to sit up competently, and balance without tumbling. "I bet I can do that," I guessed. "After all, they have support handrails, don't they?" But if I couldn't negotiate sitting up, traveling - probably in a wheelchair - to the bathroom, and transferring to and from the toilet, the bedpan was the only alternative that I could think of.

Little did I know that for the next two weeks, I would not make it anywhere close to the bathroom which was only ten feet away from my bed.

Amidst some chronic problems, I was able to count some definite blessings.

The food wasn't as award-winning as the staff had said it was, but

AN INTRO TO THERAPY

it was decent. Having choices was the key. So I sampled everything that I could, and made mental notes on my preferences.

My bed was an amazing contraption. I became a button pusher, and soon had it figured out how to raise and lower my head and my knees, pull myself up toward the top of the bed without the chucks mover crew, and roll onto my side when my back needed a break. And I could reach most of my back to scratch it, except for a narrow section down my right side which was unreachable from any direction with just one hand.

The staff was very cool about visitors, and although I knew I couldn't sponsor a late show party, they allowed Barbara to stay as late as she wanted. I did have a fairly nice flat screen TV, my own remote, and could watch movies and shows all night if I wanted to.

Within twenty-four hours, they had me scheduled for daily therapy. I was to learn the difference between a Physical Therapist and an Occupational Therapist. These were abbreviated as PT and OT. The PT was focused more on gross motor movement, walking, and getting from place to place. The OT was more focused on skill sets as they pertained to daily functionality and living needs, such as dressing, washing, and hygiene stuff. That being said, the jobs overlapped a lot, and at times they had me do identical exercises. Both had the same ultimate objective – to improve my ability to move and take care of myself.

The difference among doctors, nurses, and therapists was huge. Some doctors were encouraging, but most were dry, matter-of-fact, and often cold. Nurses were caretakers, and had their extensive checklists of "to dos" and things to research, all for the conditional security and welfare of the patient. Therapists seemed to work more independently for the general hospital staff, and were not held particularly accountable by doctors for results or reports.

ROLAND'S STORY

As my journey began, I was totally controlled by the words of the doctors who were not in most cases very positive regarding recovery. I suppose in their efforts not to be misleading and generate false hope, they tended to be "realistic," and pragmatists. As a result, discussions with doctors usually left me feeling down and victimized. Whereas, a session with a therapist left me feeling encouraged and hopeful, and usually a bit exhausted. My tendency was to smile at doctors, listen intently to what they had to say, and be happy that they didn't add bad news to my day. Therapists, on the other hand, although I wasn't necessarily thrilled to see them, brought me the opportunity to improve my condition. So I made up my mind to always greet them warmly, and take on any challenges they suggested.

My first challenge with the PT and her assistant was simply to sit up on the side of my bed. So far, the closest I had come to sitting up was to raise myself in my mechanical bed, and not even to the extreme of which the bed was capable. The limit of its back raising included a position for which I could find no practical use. It bent me forward so far that I couldn't breathe, and I felt like a WWF wrestler had me in one of those pretzel chokeholds, giving you a view of your ankles that you never thought possible.

When my first opportunity came to work with a PT, I was anxious to see what sort of expectations they had. In my case, the PT was a fairly petite woman, accompanied by a six-foot-two-inch, must-have-been-a-football-player, PT in training.

"Hello, Mr. Takaoka." I was trying to clear my throat, which had the tendency lately of collecting yucky stuff that caused me to whisper and gurgle more than I meant to. I nodded, and kept trying to locate my voice. "I'm Virginia from the PT staff, and this is Dennis, and he'll be working with us. How are you feeling?"

I flew the okay sign with my left hand touching my thumb and

AN INTRO TO THERAPY

forefinger together, and then pointing at my throat, I continued to clear. I signed another message, this one the universal "palm toward you, fingertips to sky" gesture that could have meant "hi," "stop," or "How!" if you were some kinds of American Indian. They appropriately deciphered my signing to mean, "give me a moment while I finish gagging," and patiently waited for me to speak.

"Sorry, if I'd known you were coming I'd have turned my voice on earlier." They both smiled at my light-heartedness. "Just call me Roland."

"How do you feel about doing a little walking today?" I guess they hadn't heard.

"I'll try anything you want me to, but I doubt you'll have me walking today." I said.

"Ah, yes... you had a stroke, right?" she queried. "And it affected your..." She was inspecting my chart now. "... right side?" I nodded to save my voice. "So let's do an evaluation and see exactly where you're at." Finally, the conversation had adopted some logic, and maybe intelligence as well. "Okay, Dennis, let's get him sitting up on this side." She pointed to the right side of my bed, and they went into a series of motions that were apparently routine.

They started by leveling and lowering my bed. Then they dropped the rail that extended below my waist while lying down, so that my legs could swing to the floor when the time came. Before they had me doing anything major, they did an assessment of ability to feel light touch in my arm and leg, whether I was numb anywhere, and checked to see if I could actually move any part of my right side. Virginia gently took my right arm in a two-handed grip controlling my elbow and wrist, and said, "Okay, tell me if you feel any pain whatsoever."

She proceeded to test my wrist and elbow flexibility, and started

ROLAND'S STORY

to check my range of motion at the shoulder. She moved my arm for a few seconds, and said, "Wow, so you have a lot of tone in your bicep and forearm." Basically, because of muscles involuntarily constricting, she couldn't easily straighten my arm.

"Okay, let's help him sit up."

They instructed me to reach over and grab the handrail that was still raised, protecting the upper half of my body from falling to the floor, and pull myself first onto my right side. Then from this position, they said they would gently guide my legs to the floor as I pushed the top half of my body into a sitting position. Although I understood the instruction, I could not comply. My body was much weaker than I thought. It took Dennis to support my upper body at the shoulder and Virginia guiding my legs over the side of the bed as I continued tugging and pushing at the rail, and finally I was sitting up.

Dennis kept a hand on my shoulder, and I sat awkwardly hunched over, head above my thighs. I felt light-headed, not exactly dizzy. It couldn't be the altitude. The bed raised me up this high all the time for meals. It must have been that for the first time since the stroke I was unsupported above the waist. It was exhilarating, in a way. I wanted to scratch my back. I thought about asking for the terry cloth towel treatment, and wondered if they would have any idea what I was talking about.

"Okay, try to sit up as best you can, shoulders back, back straight..." Virginia paused, assessing the results as I did my best to comply. Dennis gradually removed his hand from my shoulder, the way you'd release your fingers from the last move when building a house of cards. I was okay for about three seconds, after which I slowly but surely started to tip over back on my right side. He caught me before I went too far, and they continued to test my balance.

"Yeah, I think we'll save walking for later." said Dennis. "Now that

AN INTRO TO THERAPY

we know where we stand, we can take baby steps." Was it just me? Or was he purposely teasing me with his select choice of words? I looked at Dennis, and after a second or two, realized that he had no ill intentions, nor was he making a poor stab at comic relief. Virginia's eyes raised a bit, and she breathed a sigh, but did not respond right away. Then, she spoke.

"What we'll focus on is getting you stronger and regaining your balance. What people do not realize when they've had a stroke is that there are muscles that are affected that are not obvious, such as your back and shoulder muscles, and your abdomen. That's why you lost your balance. Your hip and torso are weak, too, and not just your leg and arm." Virginia was bringing to mind an important point. I couldn't accurate assess the extent of the damage caused by the stroke. It was going to be a long, drawn out process of discovery.

"Well, that's enough for today. We'll be back tomorrow and work on sitting up techniques." They helped me to lay down again, and suddenly I felt like I'd been practicing for a triathlon. "We'll be back tomorrow morning."

"I'll be here!" I said, not really attempting the sarcasm on purpose. They said their goodbyes, and unceremoniously marched for the door. I guess, for them, it was on to the next victim... er, patient.

After some sessions with the therapists, I gathered that, although they were focused on patients' recovery, this was still a job to them. Eight hours a day – check in... one or two patients an hour... break... therapy... lunch... therapy... break... therapy... check out. If they attended to ten or twelve patients a day, they were done. Then, within a few days cycle, any given patient left either for home, or was assigned to further rehabilitation by their insurance company. The OTs and PTs didn't step too far outside their required realm of clinical treatment.

ROLAND'S STORY

I had to wonder what they did when they had a particularly difficult patient who had an attitude. I didn't get to see them in that scenario yet.

But only weeks away, there was a completely different experience coming my way that would be enlightening. In a huge way…

6

INSIGHTS TO CHILDBIRTH

Meanwhile, the hospital administrators were dealing with my hospitalization case. Being self-employed, and struggling to help cover rent, I was without insurance. So, a fairly large bill was accruing, for which I was going to be liable.

Then some kind genius, and I never figured out who, said that I was eligible for Medi-Cal, and that all I had to do was apply, and submit the kind of documents that were going to be difficult to gather, but not impossible.

One thing that I needed was my social security card. I hadn't seen it for years. You don't think you're going to need it until you retire, and the way I was going, I hadn't considered starting to plan for it yet.

There were other required documents: taxes, proof of residence, and other account information. I was somehow able to come up with everything, while trying to get everything into the hands of the right people. This proved to be quite a task. Although it seemed

ROLAND'S STORY

to be a simple objective, this wasn't going to be fast or smooth. It would end up taking weeks.

The normal protocol for hospitalization was usually a week long process. First, stabilize patient. Then assess the best options for treatment. Whatever could be done outside of the hospital was left for the patient to negotiate with his personal doctor, referrals, and insurance companies. Then, often by the one week mark, the patient was released to go home, or do whatever they were going to do, with the added instruction to go to the emergency immediately if they should have their symptoms repeat.

As it was, my vitals were more under control. The doctors had adjusted my meds, and determined this new combination should serve me well. I didn't have any great degree of confidence in their decision. I had been taking my last combination of meds religiously when I wound up in emergency again. I really wanted some assurance that things were different this time. Yet, I couldn't find anything that would boost my confidence level.

The big difference this time was that I couldn't walk. Previously, in my past two strokes, I hadn't been reduced to a condition of not being able to stand. At least I had a weak ability to move my damaged arm. So, I went from moderate impairment to full recovery in a matter of weeks. I started showing signs of immediate improvement, and it just got better and better. This time, in two weeks even with therapy, I had gained no ground, other than generally getting some of my strength back.

Barbara and I lived in a condo close by. The problem was obvious – we lived upstairs.

Barbara had been able to buy the condo with the help of low interest rates and a recession that was hurting nearly everyone we knew. But it was without my help, because my credit was so poor I couldn't help her buy. Due to a President sanctioned tax credit and a marvelous real estate agent, along with a parent co-signer, Barbara magically qualified.

We had chosen an upstairs location with a big front patio, vaulted ceilings, and a connected garage, along with a set of carpeted stairs leading down to it. Now that we had a home we loved, it had become a huge problem for us. It wasn't safe for me to be immobile, and living upstairs was decidedly an increased hazard. To top it off, Barbara's job required her to manage a pharmacy and retail store, sometimes at six o'clock in the morning. She'd be gone all day, and there was no way I could take care of myself if they sent me home now.

One day Reggie walked in and introduced me to another doctor. "Hey Roland, how're you doing?"

"Good," I responded cheerily, seeing my friend.

"Roland, this is Dr. Wendell, and he will be overseeing your treatment when you move out of emergency. He'll take good care of you."

"Hello, Doctor." I shook his hand. He may have said something, but it was so softly spoken, I wasn't sure. Minor pleasantries regarding racquetball followed, which I doubted made any impression on Dr. Wendell. Apparently he was one of the dry ones. When they left, I thought about how different two doctors could be. Reggie was so vibrant and open, and Dr. Wendell was quiet and reserved. I got the impression that Dr Wendell was kind of weak. It disturbed me a little that he was to be in charge of my care. I guess impressions can be radically wrong, for before I left Saint Michael's, Dr. Wendell was to become the local town hero.

I did see a lot of Deana. She worked most days, and in between, several others alternated day shifts. The night nurses would come

ROLAND'S STORY

in after 7:00 PM or so, and leave about 7:00 in the morning. Hence, I saw less of them, occupying my time in visiting with Barbara, an occasional visitor, and sleeping. So, as odds would have it, Deana was the nurse on duty as my dilemma regarding constipation grew worse.

A couple of nurses had accommodated me with a bed pan, and I got to practice positioning myself precariously on an odd-shaped plastic bowl that was designed to capture virtually any mess that occurred. I personally had my doubts. The pressure building in my lower regions of my gut led me to believe that I needed something much bigger. Prior to the event, I was plagued with fears of potential mishaps. I couldn't possibly, in the history of hospitals everywhere, be the first one to suffer from this problem. These sessions ended with no success, and I continued to wait for relief.

It had been almost four days, and now I was genuinely concerned. Not only was there the unreasonable time lapse since my last bowel movement back at the condo, but now I had a constant discomfort from the increasing matter in my body that was supposed to be just passing through, and not having an extended stay.

The couple of times I had tried the bedpan, I experimented with giving a push. I was envisioning a pregnant woman at the moment of childbirth having a similar issue, although in her case the expected outcome couldn't be compared to mine. But I guess with my weak arm and leg came some other body muscles that were also weakened. I hadn't the strength or muscular coordination to have a successful maneuver. So, each time, I had to ask to have the bed pan removed with no luck. I thought perhaps that, this being more than likely one of the most undesirable tasks of a nurse or a nurse's aid, they would welcome my failure. The fact that no one around might be rooting for me was disheartening.

INSIGHTS TO CHILDBIRTH

But then, there was Deana. She seemed to be on my team no matter what the challenge. "You know, we've got to do something to help you out. I don't think the oral colase is enough."

"So, we're going to need the suppository after all?" I queried, thinking that I was already sure of her answer. But I was slightly short of the mark.

"Even that may not be sufficient. We can try it, though. If it doesn't work, I may have to help it along a bit."

Was it just me, or was a smile growing on Deana's face? Now she had my attention, with my thoughts driven by an imagination that was resisting, but being overpowered by visions of impossible potential possibilities of Deana volunteering to "help it along a bit." I rushed to exhaust all the options before she was allowed to add definition to that phrase.

"Well, let's try the suppository, for sure!" I felt like I had invited her into a private, secret corner of my life, with little left to be kept for myself. It was a final desperate attempt at keeping some dignity.

"I'll be right back," Deana responded decisively. My natural defense level had escalated to DEFCON 3, and it seemed that war was inevitable.

I mulled it over in my mind. I had to get past this. I felt as though I was in need of an operation, and indeed, a caesarean extraction began seeming plausible, and even preferable, to the advancing plot. But I was miserable, and had to believe that the remedy was easier than the problem as it was developing.

Deana returned, and prepared to administer the suppository. She had to access my files on the computer, and then add notes to my chart. Then she snapped on a pair of gloves. Deana tore open a bubble pack, releasing a large red ovalish object about an inch long. Time's up.

ROLAND'S STORY

"Okay, roll over!" said Deana.

I was getting stronger, and pretty easily reached, grabbed the rail on the right side of the bed, and submitted my backside like a bad boy about to take his spanking. But surprisingly, it was quick, painless, and not at all as invasive as I had anticipated.

"Alright, that's it. Now we wait a while." Deana couldn't have been more gracious about performing the task of inserting the suppository, and some of my anxiety was passing. "It could take an hour or more, so just let me know if you need the bedpan."

It was now dinner time, but the thought of eating was so thoroughly unacceptable that I had the kitchen delivery staff member put the tray to one side and out of sight. I believed I was about as miserable as I could get, but I was about to be schooled in human tolerance of pain.

It was a full two hours later when I called for the nurse. Earlier, Deana had poked her head in and said she was off, and there would be a changing of staff. I should have been relieved that the "Deana fantasy," or rather, "horror story," would not be allowed to play out, but my condition had pushed me way beyond any possible relief without the suppository completing its mission. It was another friendly nurse, possessed of a more passive, clinical demeanor, who responded to my summons.

Phyllis came into my room. "Hi. How's it going?"

My voice showed my stressed condition. "Phyllis, I need a bedpan right away." My gaze was unable to focus on her as she rallied to my rescue, slipping on the plastic gloves with the familiar "snap," passing hurriedly in and out of the bathroom, and collecting a bed pan as she went. I could tell she was on final approach, and prepared myself by grabbing the rail.

Phyllis said, "Okay, roll…" I pulled myself onto my side as she

INSIGHTS TO CHILDBIRTH

positioned the bed pan. "And back down..." With expert skill, she held the bedpan in place so when returning onto my back, I was now perfectly over the bedpan. "Is that good?"

"Yeah, thanks." I sort of spit out the syllables.

"Okay, so I'll leave you alone for a bit. But call if you need me."

My eyes were closed. "Uh huh," I said, as she left to offer some privacy.

What happened next would have been well described as an exorcism. Undeniably, although I had never had the experience, I knew I was about to complete the process of a successful application of a colase suppository. But no stretch of my vivid imagination could have prepared me for what was coming.

I had the sudden uncontrollable urge to push, and amazingly, I had the presence to think, "...it IS like child birth... now I know what women go through..." This was joined by a body cramp that focused all its energy toward my backside, and caused me to emit a long growl as I engaged in clenching my teeth, my fists, and belly crunching, believing that I would burst a blood vessel in my head at any second, and thinking, "This can't be right."

But it was too late. I truly believed that this whole episode was going to cost me dearly, and end in a new catastrophe.

Suddenly, there was action. Not quite the explosion that I had thought was coming, but the definitive elimination of that which had been impacted inside me and denying passage to anything through that doorway. It must have taken forty-five seconds. I was allowed time enough to get a couple breaths, then the whole thing repeated itself. I couldn't imagine that there was anything left.

The relief was incredible. I lay there with my eyes closed, not caring to move. Maybe fifteen minutes had passed, when Phyllis stepped and paused just past the doorway to the room.

ROLAND'S STORY

"How're you doing?"

All I could do was raise my left hand up off the bed, elbow still resting against me, and do the universal hand sign for success. With my hand failing to form even a poor example of a fist, I managed to extend my thumb and point it in the general direction of "up."

Phyllis received the message. "Oh, good! I'll be right there to take care of it."

I heard the unmistakable snap of plastic gloves.

7

THE CLOSEST THING TO DESOLATION

Barbara made it in late that evening, having had to work late. It was almost eleven o'clock by the time she eased in the doorway, leaning to peek in. I had already been sleeping for a few hours, having recovered enough by nine to munch a bit of cold dinner, then return to snooze. She was there long enough to make sure I was okay, and I assured her that somehow I had survived without suffering an aneurysm.

Nothing I could have said would have accurately told the tale of my ordeal, so I passed it off as, "I finally had a movement, and it was a real hassle..." and left the rest to her imagination.

"I don't think I've ever had to deal with that. I'm so sorry, baby."

"Don't worry. At least we know the remedy works." I changed the subject. "What's in the bag?" Barbara had brought in a grocery bag which I figured contained another collection of thoughtful things

ROLAND'S STORY

I might need, or maybe more of my sugar-free chocolates, or some treat to make a day a little more enjoyable.

"I got you more turtles and snack bars..." She trailed off as she rummaged through the bag.

Then Barbara pulled out a more cumbersome container that looked like it was designed for a cake, but was actually the plastic molded see-through carrier for cookies from the grocery store, arranged in a pinwheel display. They certainly weren't for me. Grocery store bakeries didn't make sugar-free cookies that I was aware of.

"I brought them to give to the nurses," she said.

Barbara was always thinking of ways to acknowledge and honor people. "They all seem so nice. I thought you could offer them as snacks and after dinner." It was Barbara's way of appreciating them. Also, if it could keep them a little bit more upbeat when their rounds brought them to my room, it couldn't hurt to be memorable.

It was late, so we made the conversation short. As Barbara was about to leave, Phyllis popped in to check on me.

"Hi, Phyllis! Got something for ya!" Barbara opened the lid of the cookie tray. "Chocolate chip cookies! Have a couple. Just a snack to get you through."

"Oh my gosh! Thank you! What a treat." Phyliss was truly surprised. She acted as if she should check with hospital protocol to see if she was allowed to accept. Or, maybe she wanted to take a cookie, but was contemplating whether the action called for rubber gloves. She hesitated ever so slightly with her hand starting a reaching maneuver. Then she cast aside her concerns and took two cookies.

As late as it was, they stood there chatting like it was a cocktail party. For a brief couple of minutes, Phyllis ignored her duties.

"You're here pretty late. Did you work tonight?" Phyllis inquired.

THE CLOSEST THING TO DESOLATION

"Yes, I closed the store tonight. This was as soon as I could get here," Barbara answered.

"My goodness, you're here like every day, aren't you?"

Barbara nodded. "I'm just trying to do everything I can for Roland. I know that he's getting weary of all this. I just can't go home without checking in on him."

"Well, don't worry," Phyliss assured her. "We'll take good care of him."

"I know you will. And thank you so much." Barbara always talked to the nurses as if being there with me was a choice as opposed to a duty. If nothing else, her attention caused them to have a little happier attitude when they came into my room. I wasn't a grouch, and I got along famously with the staff. But there was no doubt, she made my presence as a patient more memorable.

Soon after, Barbara left for the evening. But not before leaving a distinct impression on my night nurse. It appeared that we were both well-liked, if that term was applicable to a patient and his wife. Barbara's thoughtfulness definitely made a difference.

The following morning Phyllis was getting ready to finish her shift. Dr. Wendell was making early rounds that morning when Phyllis greeted him.

"Hi, Dr. Wendell."

"Good morning. Just checking how our web designer is doing."

"Oh, he's good. But you know, I've got to tell you. His wife is something else." The doctor stood quietly listening. "She worked all day, and then was here like at eleven o'clock, bringing us cookies and taking care of Roland."

"Bringing YOU cookies?" He asked, sort of surprised.

"Yes, us. He's diabetic – they sure weren't for him." Her statement left Dr. Wendell thinking as he came into my room, and saw that I

ROLAND'S STORY

was sleeping. I imagine he was perfectly in his comfort zone as he silently checked my chart, and then moved onto the next patient.

Deana came into my room after the changing of shifts, and by that time I was awake. "How's my buddy doing?"

"Fantastic!" I felt an upbeat energy in my voice.

She smiled. "So it worked?" We both knew what she was talking about.

"Man, did it!" I answered.

Deana was genuinely pleased. "Ah, I'm glad it did. I know that it can be a real problem. Lots of stroke patients get constipated."

I guess I expected her to have been mildly disappointed that she wasn't here to finish the job, or "take me to the next level." But, in any case, I was wrong.

Deana went about her usual processes – checking my temperature, taking my pulse and blood pressure, and asking the usual hospital questions that made me believe they all thought I might be crazy as well as physically impaired.

"Can you tell me your name? Your age? What day is this?" This line of questioning was going to continue for weeks. What was the point? They knew who I was. I followed along with the sport to keep the peace.

Then I realized something. Deana was simply a really sweet, warm, and friendly nurse who loved helping people. My warped vision of Deana as a sado-masochistic diva of the dark was dashed forever, and I knew I trusted her. It was hard to make friends as a patient in a hospital setting. But I had made one in Deana.

More than a week had gone by. Staff members were returning from their couple of days off, expecting to see a new face staring at them from the bed. "Hi! You're still here?" The question was going to get stale from redundant application. I soon caught on that it was highly unusual to be a patient in the stroke section of Saint Michael's Hospital for any more than seven days.

They were trying to figure out what to do with me. The fact of the matter was that if they sent me home, I was in trouble. I couldn't walk. I lived upstairs, and Barbara would be gone nine or more hours a day, five days a week.

Later that morning, I had a visit from Dr. Wendell. Man, he needed an infusion of life. His presence never rose higher than neutral, and I got the feeling he was one of those people who somehow got misplaced. "I should have been a brain surgeon!" That sort of thing. As a brain surgeon he wouldn't have to talk to people much, and he'd get paid top dollar. He just didn't seem happy. Because of that, I just couldn't imagine him bringing me tidings of comfort or joy. Today was going to be no different.

"Let's review your situation at home." He was his usual soft spoken, bland self. "You live in an apartment?"

"Condo."

"You renting?"

"No, we own." The condo was in Barbara's name. We weren't going anywhere.

"Oh, I see. One story? Downstairs?"

"No, upstairs."

"Oh... okay. Wife works?"

"Five days a week."

He paused. "Anybody else at home?

"Not really. Yes, but he's a student in school… College."

"Family living close by?" Now he was reaching.

"All up north, central Cal."

"Arg..." He was getting a little frustrated.

"Someplace you can move to for a while?" He was reaching again.

ROLAND'S STORY

"Not really, Doc."

"Crap. Well, we can't really keep you here much longer. We're exhausting our excuses. You've gotta figure something out."

It was the most emotion I was to get from Dr. Wendell. Yet, he seemed only mildly distressed.

"We're researching Medical options, but I don't think your application is complete. Well, give it some thought. Gotta figure something out. I'll see you tomorrow."

We'd talked to the agent for the hospital that dealt with insurance. I didn't have any. Medi-Cal represented a messy process that was denied to me twice before. I saw no reason why this time would be different.

It appeared to still be on me to "figure something out." I had a lot to figure out. If I went home, getting up the stairs was only the first challenge. I couldn't sit up straight on my own, I couldn't get myself out of bed, and I couldn't get myself to the toilet. That was just for starters. If I was bedridden, there was no way Barbara was going to be able to care for me. She often came home from work exhausted with sore, swollen knees or a bad back or both. Then when she was at work, we would have to deal with food, drink, cleaning, and other domestic basics. We were already being scheduled with doctors' follow up visits. Add the preparation, travel, and going up and down seventeen steps. Nothing was easy or convenient about my condition, even if I remained in the hospital and they wanted to send me home.

I wasn't sure what to think. In several churches I had attended in the past, the common line I'd be handed was equally of no use, as telling me that I "gotta figure something out."

"Let's take a moment and pray." That was it, the answer to any and every problem. Then we'd join hands, the minister would say a few words, and hand the problem, lock, stock, and barrel, over into God's hands, and let Him figure something out.

THE CLOSEST THING TO DESOLATION

At that point, it wasn't enough to hand it over to God. I wanted to do my part. The passage kept popping into my mind, "The Lord helps he who helps himself." I couldn't help myself. I was, for all intents and purposes, helpless. Needy. That thought was killing me.

I had always been known for my positive attitude. It made me happy when people were lifted by talking to me. But at this point, I was the one in need of positivity. I had to feel like there was something I could do. Each day, I faced the world of "can'ts," when only a little over a week ago, I "could." My world had narrowed down so radically that an inventory of "can do's" would only take a couple of minutes.

For the first time, I gave in to feeling sorry for myself. If I knew that I could get better, it would be so much easier to do my thing with diligence and have patience while it took however long it took. But no one could tell me for sure that I would walk again. No one could guarantee me a timeline.

"The Lord helps he who helps himself." The words kept reverberating in my mind. It was a Biblical saying I'd always believed. It made sense not to sit on your duff and plead for mercy, when you could make some kind of an effort. It's just that I never had so little that I could do.

It was at that point that I lost it. My grip on hope caved in. Barbara was hanging tough, but no one with any clout or authority was being merciful enough to toss me a lifeline.

I reached over, grabbed the rail of the bed, pulled myself over to my right side, covered my head with my pillow, and cried until I passed out a couple hours later.

8

A MESSAGE IN THE NIGHT

That day, Barbara had been called to work early, and yet she had to close the store on top of that. People would call in sick, and sometimes they actually were sick.

She had called the nurse on duty, and sent a verbal message. I knew she'd come, but it would be later. So, she had altered her original plan to drop by and see me late morning, and said it would be more like nine or later. She responded to the call to come into work early on the premise that she could move her shift time up, and get off earlier than scheduled... which never happened, because, again, someone else called in sick. Again, it was edging in on eleven o'clock when she got to my hospital room.

For a second night she leaned into the room, as if only showing her head and upper body had less of a chance of waking me if I were asleep. Still lying on my right side, not willing to move, my eyes were open and staring at the wall. The tears had stopped, but not my quandary over what to do about my situation. I still felt helpless.

A MESSAGE IN THE NIGHT

"Oh, hi baby! Why aren't you asleep?" She smiled and stood straighter as she walked in.

I rolled my body onto my back, and stretched my left arm. At least if my eyes were swollen it might look like a result from sleeping. "I was... just happened to be awake when you popped your head in."

"I won't stay long, but wanted to see if you were okay." The smile was there, but her walk betrayed her weariness. We gave each other a peck on the lips, and she held my face in both her hands. There was never a question about how much I was loved. Barbara was perhaps the only one whose attitude was consistently confident that I would get better. She was working the hardest to keep focused on the positive.

We chatted a little while longer, and I acted as if I were about to drift. Barbara took advantage of the clue and opted to say goodnight. We said our "I love you's," and she quietly took leave. It had been a week of emotional ups and downs, but until today I had managed to keep the dips fairly shallow. This evening I was flat-lining on an all-time low, and I was glad not to have to converse and try to act congenially while my thoughts were so dark.

I was so tired of hearing doctors talk about status quo versus getting well, and they seemed to be adjusting to my state, rather than hoping that I'd recover.

I started feeling resentful and angry. What was their agenda? Was their policy to "error on the side of hopeless" just in case I didn't get better? I relied on them for guidance, and needed to have them looking for answers, and not settling.

It seemed like they were fine with my condition as long as I didn't get worse. Even the therapists acted satisfied focusing on me adjusting my expectations to "my new condition." I wanted them to "make a startling discovery," the way doctors do, or find a new procedure

ROLAND'S STORY

that could awaken the nerve connections in my right appendages. I wanted them to be expecting a miracle, not taking notes on "what was." I needed them to be searching for possibilities, not settling for averages. I was desperate for my team to rally for a touchdown, and not simply wait to block the next kick.

"C'mon guys! I'm in your hands!" But who was I talking to? What was their stake?

No one appeared willing to stick their neck out. Instead of a pat on the shoulder, I wanted a helping hand to pick me up, but it apparently wasn't available. I began wondering why people became doctors, nurses, and even therapists. What I was experiencing was an all too vivid example of an entire occupational community transforming its enthusiastic, energized newbies into disappointed, seasoned realists, no longer struggling against the binds of the system. It reminded me of the school system and its processing of new teachers aspiring to "help young minds," into weary wardens of the short term inmates, intent only upon keeping their jobs and pensions.

I guessed that if I wanted hope I was going to have to find a preacher, and one who believed in miracles, as opposed to one prone to talking about Satan's gleeful campaign to take control over the souls of humanity.

It was in this grim state of mind that I finally did slip into slumber land, with my thoughts still questioning the legitimacy of the medical industry becoming a field in which the prime skill was breaking bad news to sick people.

... and I dreamed ...

> *I was walking... how cool... there were people all around walking different directions. Mostly young people. It reminded me a lot of my high school days. That was when I started my philosophical lean towards learning.*

A MESSAGE IN THE NIGHT

... everything changes ... nothing stays the same ... facts are relative ... all paths lead to the same destination ...

I walked up to some people setting up tables. On the tables they placed trays of cookies and cakes and more. It was a bake sale. I knew I could find something I'd like. There were voices, ladies chatting and giving setup orders. Reviewing the choices, I selected a pastry, pointed at it, and was asked by the lady helping me, "Would you like a bag?" I nodded yes. She turned and looked for one. As I waited, the pastry, and anything like it, seemed to be no longer available. Now, the lady wasn't looking for a bag, but a pastry like the one that I had asked for. "How about a cookie? Piece of Cake?" Neither looked particularly appetizing. I passed, having set my sights on the pastry, nothing else appealed to me. I was disappointed, and did not want to settle...

I kept walking. There were rows of buildings with brown walls. Lockers. Grass between the buildings. Nobody to recognize ... It really did look like my high school. Those were the days when my mind was less cluttered. Life was easier...

... A tiny monkey appeared. What was he wearing ... was it a kimono? Silly. He even looked like an Asian philosopher ... the simian sensei ... in my dream, I was oddly aware that I was dreaming. "Okay – I'll go along." I thought to myself.

My knees were worn out in real life, and no better in my dream state. I awkwardly got down on a meager patch of dry grass, and sat across from the monkey. The monkey held out his right hand, palm up, as if expecting me to give him something. All I could think of was to copy the gesture with my left hand. The monkey's hand was only large enough to grasp me by the index finger. As if examining my finger print he concentrated for a few seconds. Then, releasing my finger, he placed his hands

ROLAND'S STORY

together kind of like an opera singer preparing to vocalize, and sighed as if his decision of what to say had been made.

His miniature size did not limit his lifelike and humanesque appearance. When the monkey began speaking, it was not loud, yet in my mind his clarity of tone and meaning were unmistakable.

"Seek not what others seek. Seek what you seek first." For the following few seconds everything remained in place ... then my vision started to fade... the profound message lingering.

I awakened with a start. The lights were low. As if I had just magically walked the campus of my old high school, my memory was perfect. I expected the images of cookies, cakes, pastries, and a miniature monkey guru to soon fade from memory like so many random dreams. But the movie replayed from memory as perfectly as a video, right down to the sore knees, a fancy-robed monkey, and the impossibly spoken words - "Seek not what others seek. Seek what you seek first."

It must have been after midnight. I lay motionless wondering what had just happened. It took me a few minutes to realize that my recall of the entire dream was exact. This had never happened to me before. I could often remember brief dream segments or faces, but never the composite sequences of an entire episode.

Fifteen minutes later they were still there. I hadn't moved. It left me with the distinct impression that I'd just had an oddly unique experience, like stepping into a parallel universe, and stepping back again. I could sense nothing ominous about the dream, and could not relate its content to anything in recent memory that could have spawned so unusual a plot. It had me baffled.

I kept running the line from the monkey over and over. "... seek what you seek first." The words felt significant. "Seek not what others

A MESSAGE IN THE NIGHT

seek." What was it that others were seeking? For that matter, what did I seek?

For a time I was unburdened from my feeling of helplessness by the riddle of the talking monkey. I gave in to a much needed rest that was free from my troubles, and replaced with several hours of dreamless sleep.

9

I DISCOVER WHAT'S EXPECTED OF ME

The memory of the dream was still with me the next day. The riddle of the words persisted, but had taken on no deeper meaning. Gaining full alertness, I intended to focus more mental energy upon the problem.

I had to consider what source had generated such a message. Most dreams were instigated by a state of mind, a life experience, or maybe a need, either philosophical or real. A dream could be an expression of psychological need, or an expectation, or fear. But I couldn't seem to attach a value to it. Obviously I needed to research this.

I decided that I needed my laptop computer in order to pursue an education on the subject of dreams. It was a good idea anyway, so that I could get to almost two weeks of emails, contact people, and let the important ones know that I was alive and kicking... with one foot, anyway.

The downer moment that I had had the evening before was less

I DISCOVER WHAT'S EXPECTED OF ME

of a subject on my mind. I wasn't one to cater to depression, or complain incessantly about life. Although it wasn't easy to ignore my environment and my condition, a computer with Internet access would at least be a great distraction.

Hey! Couldn't I watch Netflix online? Now I was sold! There were a multitude of movies I could watch, and even check out some series from TV that people said were so good, but that I had never heard of from being without TV service. And hell, it wasn't like I had to keep appointments, or attend networking events. Maybe I could even try a bit of web design. I wouldn't be fast, but I could do it. For my work, my brain mattered way more than my dexterity.

That evening, Barbara came in as usual, and agreed that the laptop was a great idea, and made plans to bring it to me the next day. The advent of the Internet had provided me ways to keep in touch with family and friends, allowed me to self-train for a new occupation, and even handed me a way to keep working if I was hospitalized. It tripped me out to think of the virtual universe that was my life.

I contemplated whether I would retain the details of my dream. It was still available for instant playback in my mind whenever I wanted. But most of the time I forgot my dreams. Why was it different this time? I wanted to record it, but I couldn't write my name... I certainly couldn't take notes. Not until I had my computer, anyway. So I resolved to rely on my memory, and figured that if I lost track of the dream... well, there was still Netflix.

Things had ironically become routine – vitals checks every two hours; two minute visits from the doc' to see if I was walking yet; PT workout; OT workout with Marilyn; three meals a day; menu lady to take my order; peeing in a bottle; pooping in a bowl; and twice more, the dreaded red gelcap suppository of colase when the "going got tough," so to speak.

ROLAND'S STORY

After the first week, the PT got the habit of timing my therapy session just before lunch. This was good, in a way, because we had progressed from just balancing in a sitting position on the bed, to getting pretty good at transferring to a chair. I got over the dizziness that followed being suddenly upright as opposed to inclined. Also, I seemed able to take deeper breaths. But the greatest benefit was sitting up when I was served a meal, and eliminating the bib required to catch the fallout.

And suddenly, I could order soup! I wouldn't be splattering my bib with spilled spoonfuls, and having to change my gown after every meal because of the overflow.

I'd been settling for salads as a common side, because with a constipation problem, I needed to consume things that helped me out. This compelled me to focus on vegies, both fresh and cooked, and of course the one product on their menu of which I was otherwise least likely to ever partake – prunes. If I never had to eat another after I got out of the hospital, I'll probably die happy.

Sitting inclined in a bed presented an issue for the consumption of soup. It was an insane challenge to attempt the use of what they referred to as a spoon, when it held so little that a starving man would perish from malnutrition before successfully feeding himself a bowl of soup. Hospitals, operating on a budget, provided pieces of plastic that sort of resembled eating utensils, but fell way short of the mark in practicality. Furthermore, for the sake of cleanliness, a sanitized fork, knife, and spoon, accompanied each meal tray, complete with a napkin only large enough to wipe your mouth maybe twice, and wrapped in a sealed plastic pouch that was difficult to open with two hands, let alone one.

I'll describe these utensils one at a time.

The fork. Half the size of a normal fork, and very little could

I DISCOVER WHAT'S EXPECTED OF ME

balance on it. Useless as a food cutting tool, the tangs were thin and weak, and tended to bend on contact, often springing food off the plate, and perhaps off the tray. Hence, the bib.

The knife. Designed more solidly than the fork, and capable of sawing through any kind of food the kitchen could put on a plate... as long as it could be held in place. In my case, without a second hand to hold the "spring-fork" and steady the object, my knife worked alone, and the larger chunks shoved other food off my plate, and sometimes the tray. Hence, the bib.

The spoon. Made with identical structural integrity as the fork, and could hold perhaps a quarter of a teaspoon of liquid if perfectly balanced. Best application for practical use of this implement was as a coffee stir stick, because it was impossible to transport anything more than a few inches without spilling. Hence, the bib.

The utensils were not the only obstacles to successful food consumption. Although the chefs reportedly maintained high ratings regarding the quality of their food and nutrition, there were still the factors of edibility and appeal. There was the "string bean" syndrome, and other relative issues such as bell peppers and onions cut in long, inconvenient strips, broccoli in chunks too large to fit in my mouth; and cauliflower, also too large, that resisted both fork stabs and knife slashes, and refused to be balanced on any utensil.

There were chicken breasts, roast beef slices, and pork chops, all of which needed cutting. There was salad served in a Styrofoam bowl with a two inch base that was definitely not designed to hold anything. There was sliced melon served in a tall cup, strawberries that, when stabbed, wouldn't stay on the fork, and grapes... well, you can just imagine. They turned out to be the easiest fruit, because I just picked them up and popped them in my mouth, and wiped my hand on my bib, because by then I didn't have a napkin. There were

ROLAND'S STORY

noodle pastas in meat sauce, lasagna, macaroni n' cheese, and garlic bread, all of which I wasn't supposed to eat because I was diabetic.

In order to improve my culinary experience, I applied every form of condiment I could get my hand on. There was creamer for coffee, sugar-free jelly for toast, syrups, fake butter, honey, all of which came sealed in mini-tubs that were nearly impossible to open one-handed. I eventually figured out techniques to accommodate my challenges effectively. I resigned myself to eating my food cold because of taking so long to prepare. It was going to become a tradition that the CNA's, or nurses' aids, would walk in forty minutes after setting me up for a meal, see a plate of food that had hardly been touched, and turn around and walk out, bothered by having to reschedule the tray cleanup.

About the time of dinner being served, and I was engaged in my tradition of preparing a cold dinner, when Barbara was nearly at my doorway, Marilyn, the OT happened to be finishing up with another patient in a nearby room. She had met Barbara previously, and when she saw her she smiled. At the same time, Barbara's gaze found Marilyn, and her face went from the ever-constant light smile that was effortless, to the beaming, bright infusion of joy. I had been telling Barbara about the therapist lineup who were a part of my treatment, and Marilyn's name had come up repeatedly. Occasionally, Barbara had seen her in passing, so she knew who she was. "Hi, you're Marilyn! I'm Roland's wife. How are you doing today?" She was happy to meet the lady who had made such an impression on me.

"Great! Thanks for asking. I know who you are. Good to see you." I could hear both of their voices in the hallway. It was easy to recognize Barbara's voice, but I wasn't sure who she was talking to. In this environment, odds were that it wasn't an old friend. So, I guessed that she was making a new one, as she was so prone to do.

"Marilyn, I've been meaning to ask you... they're going to be sending

I DISCOVER WHAT'S EXPECTED OF ME

Roland home soon, and I'm worried. I have to learn how to help Roland transfer to and from a wheel chair, and how to do other things, because, basically, we're on our own. Could I join in one of your therapy sessions, and could you teach me the critical things I need?" Marilyn's reaction showed that this was not a common request.

"Oh, sure! I'm here until at least five almost every day. Do you have a time slot we can plan for? I'll meet you." Marilyn was quite happy to comply.

The fact was, most family members were timid about being involved with their loved ones' recoveries. Family had other issues that they were confronting, and these compounded the problem.

While a patient was trying to kick start rehab and find baby steps that were negotiable, the family members were reeling from the impact of the disability on the family unit, and battling discomfort and depression, as well as the psychological damage of being robbed of normal functionality. Family members didn't always realize that they were the pep team, and were in the best position to be supportive and encouraging, and possibly even participate.

Marilyn set a time on Barbara's next day off, and during a future therapy session would show Barbara some of the best techniques to help me move, and how to use positioning and leverage to assist in my transfers without endangering me, or hurting herself, which was just as critical an issue. Indeed, when Marilyn would complete the instruction, Barbara, would be more effective than the PT in training, Dennis. Obviously, common sense and knowledge, with proper coaching, achieved higher marks than a medical degree without these things. One could spend years getting good grades and a certificate, but apparently that did not necessarily make a good therapist. My respect would grow for Marilyn, who was raising the bar on standards for rehab personnel.

ROLAND'S STORY

Leave it to Barbara to reach out when others would not. In the hospital environment, there was no instruction book available guiding the patient or his family. It paid to ask questions, and to ask for help. It was a bonus if your request was a plea for assistance on how to be more independent.

They set a date and time, and agreed to meet. Barbara offered something from her bag, saying "I brought some candies in to share with the staff! Here, have a few. They'll give you the will to make it through the day."

As they parted, Barbara continued on to my room. But Marilyn's gears were grinding. She knew now that I was in a predicament. I needed more time, and the hospital was not going to allow it. It seemed that I was overstaying my welcome.

Just then Dr. Wendell walked by the far end of the corridor. "Oh! Dr. Wendell!" He had passed out of site, but apparently the sound waves had caught up to him. To Marilyn, she appeared to have missed him. But out of site, just past the right turn in the hallway, he had stopped dead in his tracks, and looked up at the ceiling, thinking. Did someone call his name?

Dr. Wendell took a tentative step backwards and leaned so that he could peer down the hall, just his head showing to Marilyn. Relieved that she hadn't missed him, she moved swiftly down the hall to keep him from waiting.

"Hi, Marilyn. What's the rush?" Dr. Wendell asked.

"I want to talk to you about Roland and Barbara." And she proceeded to tell him about the upcoming therapy training, Barbara's diligence in visiting me, and her overall involvement. She reported on me as a patient, saying that I was giving it one-hundred and ten percent, and that no one showed a more positive attitude.

Dr. Wendell listened. He thanked Marilyn for the information.

I DISCOVER WHAT'S EXPECTED OF ME

She stated her case that I really needed more time. When she had finished, he simply nodded acknowledgement, and thanked her. As he continued down to hall, she didn't know if the chat had been of any help. But at least she had done what she could.

Barbara came into my room loaded down with goodies. She brought with her "hello kiss" a selection of sugar-free candies, a couple of cards that I had received in the mail, and a large, black nylon bag that could only contain my laptop. In the midst of my job of tediously hacking large chunks into smaller bites, and applying dressing to salad and fake butter to my dinner roll, I stopped and cheered!

"Yay! Man, am I glad to see you! Especially 'cuz you bring goodies!" She had mentioned the day before that her intentions were to restock my supply of fun things to eat.

"Hi, Baby! And I remembered your laptop!" Barbara always brought light to the moment, no matter how low she was on her own energy. She presented me with my kiss. "I'll get it set up for you in a moment. Just let me set all this stuff down. How was your day?"

"Aw, I've just been layin' around." She sensed that I seemed to be in a decent mood. We both had a chuckle. Barbara was glad that in spite of circumstances I was trying to keep positive.

"I met with Marilyn out in the hall. She's going to teach me to assist you in transferring to a chair, and a few things." It was break through news. We were getting concerned because of my disability, and recovery was likely to take some time. But I had something on my mind that was becoming an obsession, and I had to tell her.

"I had a dream last night, and I am really anxious to read up on it, and see if I can figure out if there's a significance." I told her briefly about the wise monkey in my dream, and she humored me. We chatted during my meal, then she helped me back into bed.

ROLAND'S STORY

Barbara strong-armed me from the chair, supporting my weak side, and helped as she could to get my body and gown rearranged. The therapists had come mid-afternoon that day, so instead of sitting in a chair for lunch, it was dinner. I wasn't all that strong yet, and sitting in a chair was a chore. I was glad for the reprieve from my practice sitting.

"So, let's set up your laptop on your table, and we'll roll it over your bed." It was a great idea, and I was glad for the specially designed table on wheels that supported the table top on one end so that its length could be extended almost across the entire bed.

"Perfect." I said when Barbara was finally done connecting the power cable and arranging the laptop. We decided to try the Netflix connection. Sure enough, my laptop gave us access to our account. There were perhaps thousands of programs and movies from which to select and watch instantaneously. Barbara maneuvered a comfy high-backed chair close to the bed, and we positioned the computer so that we could both see it. We selected an action adventure that looked promising, and started the flick. Inside of ten minutes, she was asleep. I could tell from her breathing that she was deep in slumberland.

I paused the movie, and opened a new browser, and thought to myself that I was truly grateful that this hospital had Wi-Fi Internet. I accessed a search engine, and my education on dreams had begun. Barbara slept for an hour, and I spent the entire time reading on my subject.

Someone had once told me that dreams were a way of communicating with other spirits, implying a connectivity to guardian angels and relatives long gone, I supposed. Another person said something about dreams being a doorway to inner consciousness. I was pretty open-minded, and at this point I was ready for the revelation of

I DISCOVER WHAT'S EXPECTED OF ME

some long hidden secret. I got all sorts of clues from dozens of sites, some of which were fairly scientific, and others of which were akin to studying mythology. Yet, I didn't choose to throw out any ideas that might lead me to a solution to my personal puzzle.

Then I started finding things. One well-known site handed me some interesting things to think about.

> *"The word dream originates from a Middle English word, 'dreme,' which means "joy" and "music."*

That was actually kind of cool. The same site offered some other attention grabbers.

> *"Clinical tests have shown that your brain waves are more active when dreaming than when you are awake."*

That one threw me. And then, I chanced upon a page with descriptions of meanings of things that people dream about, and that's when I discovered the showstopper.

> *"The symbol of a monkey in your dream represents deceit, insight, and intuition. Those who are around you are striving to advance their own interests."*

Did this website see me coming? My puzzle had only gotten more contrived. It was as if the monkey that I had encountered in my dream was a common entity, maybe well-known in the subconscious world, and might be dropping tidbits of wise messages all over. There seemed to be too much similarity with the website's description of a potentially prophetic primate and the etheric, random, literally pint-sized monkey in my dream that had the arrogance to tell me what to seek in life.

But the monkey's message came back to me, redelivered in as

ROLAND'S STORY

perfect a display as when I'd dreamed it. "Seek not what others seek. Seek what you seek first."

The fact that I was diligently performing research on a dream that I was able to recall perfectly, and now was reading an online publication that described it, was too convicting. I had been in need of a clue. I was handed that clue. Then I had put the clue to the test, and had been given confirmation. I reread the excerpts. The hair on the back of my neck stood up, and I shivered from the tickle I felt.

What exactly was the monkey trying to tell me? Suddenly it hit me like a heavy load. I slowed my thinking so that I could mentally examine and sort the data.

Let's see...

> *My situation was fairly grim when discussed by the professionals around me, who were only concerned with 'advancing their own interests.' They didn't care about encouraging me, but were more focused on not offering me false hope, so they wouldn't have to answer to my disappointment. They'd rather have me believe that I wasn't going to get better than to take a chance by giving me something to believe in. I was seeking answers from the doctors, when they sought only not to be wrong.*
>
> *Then the monkey, the source of insight and intuition that could recognize this deceit, was telling me not to follow the doctors dead end lead, but seek what it was that I wanted first – and I wanted to get well!*

All at once I realized what had happened, and accepted it with perfect conviction. As clearly as if it had been written in a contract, I knew what was expected of me.

I had received a divine message!

I DISCOVER WHAT'S EXPECTED OF ME

"No Shit!" I exclaimed out loud, and breaking the relative silence, Barbara started from her chair.

"What Baby... good movie?" I smiled as she forced her body and mind to return from sleep mode. I said quietly, "Sweetie, I know what to do. The dream was a message from God, a guardian angel, or something. I have to quit listening to anybody who doesn't believe that I can get well, and I have to decide what to do."

"That sounds good, Baby..." Barbara stretched in her chair, extending her legs and reaching up with her arms.

I wasn't going to try to explain more about my dream world messenger. It was time to make sure that Barbara was awake enough to make it safely home for the night. I was going to sleep well that night, and most nights that followed. Perhaps I'd get a repeat visit from my monkey guru, and he would share more words of wisdom with me.

10

A LITTLE HELP HERE... AND THERE

I had been at Saint Michael's over two weeks. I kept wondering when Dr. Wendell would walk in and hand me my walking papers... uh, I guess my rolling papers. Reggie had passed through fairly regularly just to say "hi," and always had a smile and a pleasant attitude.

This morning Dr. Wendell came in after breakfast, sporting the same demeanor as he always did, his face unreadable as to whether it was a failed attempt at smiling, or a grimace.

"Hi, Roland." He had just recently stopped calling me by my last name. I wanted to interpret this as a sign that he was warming up, but could uncover no other evidence to support it. I was about to receive a moderate shock.

"I've been talking to your finance administrator about your situation, and I think we have an idea. We're trying to get your application for Medi-Cal pushed through." He delivered this information

A LITTLE HELP HERE...AND THERE

as blandly as if he were telling a patient that they weren't sure what disease he was afflicted with, and would have to run some more tests.

"I don't understand," I said, obviously puzzled. "A finance agent was just here yesterday, and said she needed tax returns, expense reports, and a couple of other things before I'd qualify, and while I'm here in the hospital, I'm not sure how to get it all together."

"I think we've found a way. Just get your bank statements for the last few months to her department, and that should do it. What do you think? Can you do that?" Was that the beginning of a smile on his face?

"Sure." I said. "I bank online, and with my laptop I can do it from this bed!"

"So, let's take care of that asap, and we'll see what happens. Okay?" Dr. Wendell held out his hand as he finished, and reversed his grip when he realized I could only reach out with my left.

"Okay, Doc, whatever you say." I answered, and gripped his hand firmly.

I didn't know whether to cheer or what. I didn't understand Medi-Cal. I just knew that it was my only chance to get help with my hospital bill. I stared after Dr. Wendell as he ambled out as quietly as he entered. Although I had thought that he was going to crack a smile and spread some joy, he fooled me again. I wondered how a guy so young for a doctor could possess such a flat personality.

Later that day, I had secured digital copies of my bank statements, and was making plans for getting them to Mrs. Sandoval, the finance administrator in charge of my application for Medi-Cal. Timing was an issue, for she was the one person with any key processing ability, but she was inundated with an overwhelming amount of work. It wasn't like I could visit the finance office, and she was only available nearly identical hours as Barbara's work schedule, so she could not

ROLAND'S STORY

do the running for me. We persisted and kept missing, until one day Dr. Wendell came again, and he had an agenda.

"How's it coming?" He asked without the usual greeting. I knew what he was asking.

"Hey, Doc'... I'm a little frustrated. Mrs. Sandoval is trying to be available, but I can't go to her, and Barbara works almost the exact office hours as she is available. We're so close, but can't pull off the touchdown." He could feel my anxiety. "I've got digital files that I emailed to her, but she says she never got them. I have print copies right here, but she'd have to come get them."

Dr. Wendell's countenance never changed. He was still stone faced and on the sour side. "Well, it sounds like it's time to squeeze a few heads. Let me have your copies." I gestured to a folder on the counter, and said, "Right there in the folder." He picked up the folder and briefly examined its contents. "Okay..." He said. "You've done your part. Let's see what we can do."

Dr. Wendell mouth a "Bye," that I really couldn't hear, and added a wave that hardly fit the category of "Greetings and Salutations." Then he was shuffling out the door, my folder in hand.

By now I was antsy about waiting for the Medi-Cal application to process. What I did know was that I would benefit financially, and that some aspect of my benefits would affect what kind of help I might receive after my release from the hospital. I had heard conversations that suggested that really top-of-the-line insurance coverage could get a benefactor months of rehabilitation in outstanding care centers. However, I hadn't had any experiences with care centers outside the hospital. Word was that patients with great healthcare coverage received better general treatment, advanced therapy, newer technology, and more time dedicated to making an impact on healing. So far, my caregivers would sometimes mention healing, but their working directives seemed more in tune with lessons on how to adjust and cope, and strengthening the muscles that worked, rather than waking up the ones that weren't.

What I really wanted was for someone to ask me what I wanted, instead of how I'm feeling. Technically, I felt stiff, sore, weak, itchy, bored, generally irritable, and periodically constipated. I guess asking me what I wanted was a dangerous thing, because I wanted to get well. I was tired of being told, "It is what it is..." and, "Brain cells don't come back..." and, "All you can do is keep trying," as a way of conveying that "it's hopeless, but keep the faith."

What I wanted was to get my body back. All of it. I wasn't prepared to settle for sixty percent. I wanted someone to tell me exactly what exercises to do to get stronger and get my lost movement back. I wanted to get the nerve endings in my brain to start talking to my deaf arm and leg. I wanted to be challenged.

I had made up my mind after absorbing the importance of my monkey dream research that I didn't care what anyone else thought about my condition. I was going to heal. What I really needed was someone besides Barbara to believe that I would heal too. I needed some kind of cheerleader. I needed a flag bearer.

Although I was willing to do whatever it took, I had to know what that was. Even if I was reaching for possibilities, I had to be reaching. If I didn't get better, it wasn't going to be for lack of trying. My goal was obvious. But there was something missing...

... I was without a battle plan.

Meanwhile, I still had therapy five days a week, and sometime six. Virginia, my PT, and trainee Dennis, still showed up as a team, with Dennis assuming more command, and Virginia observing, suggesting, and sometimes participating. Today was going to be exemplary of our daily ritual.

ROLAND'S STORY

"Hi there, Roland. Are you ready to do some more standing today?" Virginia was always pretty congenial, although she seemed disconnected somehow. It was as if I was a project, and the project had time requirements, not result requirements.

"Sure. Why not?" I wasn't totally demotivated. But I didn't care much, either. Even though I didn't have one yet, I knew that Virginia and Dennis weren't going to be a part of my battle plan.

Dennis took the lead with, "Okay, shall we work on bed to chair transfers?" He looked at Virginia for approval of his suggestion... not me. She answered, "That sounds good." I could imagine the sequence. Sit up. Bed to chair... chair to bed... back and forth, maybe three times, resting in between... end up in the chair... see ya later... sit until lunch was over.

I guess I needed this. But the process lacked creativity. It was just this tedious, tiring process that got me worn out before lunch. But it was bound to do some good. So I always put forth my best effort.

Since my strength was still subpar, the therapists used what was called a "gait belt" to assist in controlling my body. It was usually adjusted to ride above my hips and fit fairly snugly. Sometimes they set it more across my chest, depending on what we were doing. Standing practice required positioning higher up on my chest, and for transfers they often positioned the belt lower. Today, the belt was low, and Dennis' job was to attempt a solo transfer. In other words, I was the object to transfer, and he was on his own. I guess it was field testing day.

Therapists can do some remarkable things. With the right touch, and support applied strategically, even one therapist can get a physically impaired person to do what three unskilled people can't. Virginia stepped clear, and waited as Dennis designed his move.

"Okay, now I'm going to support your right knee and keep it from

A LITTLE HELP HERE...AND THERE

buckling inwards..." He faced me, bent low at the waist so that his shoulder was at my chest level, and placed his right knee between my knees, applying pressure that indeed would lock my knee from giving way and possibly causing me to fall. At the same time, he reached under my good arm, around, and firmly grasped the gait belt at the small of my back. With his left hand, he grabbed the gait belt also, so that now his arms encircled my body, his right leg rooted between both of mine, ready to lift.

Dennis gave me his last second review on techniques. "Now remember... lean way forward, get your weight above your feet, stand, pivot, and slowly sit down." I examined our construct and couldn't see the logic in his instructions in regards to our positioning. "Okay, ready?"

I said, "Wait a minute... I can't do this."

"Well, just give it a try." He thought I was wimping out on him in the midst of his test.

"No, I mean I really cannot do this, physically!" Wasn't I speaking English? Maybe he just wasn't listening.

"Sure you can! We've done it a dozen times! You can do it! C'mon!" He looked like a lineman about to toss the quarterback.

Dennis wasn't going to get it. Finally, I resigned myself. I couldn't see his vision, but after all, he was the therapist. "Ah-right..." I ventured doubtfully. We counted to three together, and we were in motion.

I made it all of about four inches, my chest pressed solidly against his shoulder. Dennis heaved with a considerable effort to help lift my body, but with his bulk immediately in front of me, my feet rooted, I simply had nowhere to go. What he expected my body to do had no chance of success without the aid of levitation or a Star Trek transporter. Realizing that it was futile, Dennis set me down. He stood back and looked puzzled, wondering what went wrong.

"I tried to explain." I said. "Positioned the way we were that just

ROLAND'S STORY

wasn't going to work." I could almost hear his gears grinding as Dennis set his mind to the task of digesting what I was feeding him. He stood motionless for a few seconds. Virginia was grinning.

I grabbed the moment to redesign the relocation project, and ease Dennis off the hook. "Let's try this. Now turn your back so that you're facing the direction we're heading. Use your other leg to brace mine... and keep your shoulder behind me, that way I'm free to reach and lean on the chair. Now let's try again. One, two, three!" I leaned forward, stood, supported myself with my left hand on the arm of the chair, pivoted smoothly, and, free of obstacles, I lowered myself neatly in the destination chair.

Dennis looked stunned. He was still figuring it out, but it was Virginia's turn to speak. She was grinning widely, and her voice was musical. "Dennis. You just got schooled by a patient!"

Dennis turned red. And so did I... for Dennis.

Several more days passed following the same trends. Dennis had misplaced some of his confident edge, replaced by a more reserved style. It was probably going to serve him well to realize that he could learn something from listening to patients.

The meals improved at times when Maria announced that the chefs had added an unscheduled alternative, like spaghetti in meat sauce, or baked ham with scalloped potatoes. I gathered that they made these special courses as a way of offering bonuses to the staff, and in making extra, they often could share with patients who were "in the know." Being the longest resident of the hospital that the staff could remember gained me privileges of sorts, and just about everyone from all shifts and all departments knew me by name.

There was one bright light added as of the last week or so. Marilyn had started visiting me as my exclusive OT once a day, every day, except Sundays. Somehow, it had been arranged that the typical

A LITTLE HELP HERE…AND THERE

rotation of therapists was superseded by her standing assignment to work with me. She was scheduled Monday through Friday. On one particular Saturday, she made some excuse to come in, casually checking her schedule, which was the same every week, or checking to see if she might have inadvertently forgotten something important the day before. So she dropped in since she was passing by.

"Hello, Roland! How's it going? Ever hear anything from Medi-Cal?" Same warm, calm personality as always.

"Marilyn, didn't you get enough of me during your work week? You just had to come see me on your day off. Don't tell me your life is that dull!" She was another member of staff who was always a pleasure. Her job was the same low expectation, daily routine as the PTs, but her attitude was different. Quite simply, she loved people, and she loved her work.

She smiled a toothy grin. "I don't believe that we reached your daily torture quota. I thought I'd fix that!"

Whereas the PT was focused on gross motor skills and being able to walk, Marilyn's job as OT was more centered on functionality for home or work, such as dressing, brushing teeth, and cleaning.

"Your hand could some extra attention. It's got a lot of tone. What do you say we give it a little stretch?" She pulled a chair close, reached for my hand, and started a conversation by asking me about how the PTs were doing with me. That opened a door to a stream of expression that had been stifled since my hospitalization. As I went on I shared with her my quandary of not understanding what was taking so long, what benefits I would gain, and what was keeping me here after an unprecedented three weeks. Changing the subject she asked about my job, my family, and my dreams. It was really refreshing just to focus on things other than my condition.

I decided that it wasn't fair that we had only been discussing me.

ROLAND'S STORY

"What about you? What do you do when you're not working, like right now?" I kidded, and we had a chuckle. She told me about her little girl and her husband, and about spending most of her off time with them.

The whole time we talked she was calmly leaning on the bed rail, holding my hand, and stroking it lightly. Although I spent a great deal of time getting my arm to relax from a retracted position across my chest, I hadn't had much luck with my hand, which performed as if it was equipped with tiny rubber bands in the joints to return it to a contorted clench. At that moment my arm felt as relaxed as it had been in three weeks, elbow on the bed, my hand open and palm down being caressed by her touch.

"Wow, you got my hand to open up. I haven't been able to do that in weeks." I noticed my whole body was relaxed. With her ministrations, I had reached a state of physical peace. Normally, any kind of movement, such as turning on my side, scratching an itch, or sitting up for a meal would result in a number of muscles on the right side of my body to spasm, resulting in an involuntary leg movement or a mild cramp somewhere. But my right arm and hand were a constant challenge to keep from continuous cramping. A sneeze or a yawn were enough to set it off.

"Good." She said. I realized that she had been distracting me with our talk while easing the tension in my hand. It had worked. It occurred to me that if I could change the automatic impulse to seize up, maybe I could also get the silent parts of my body to start talking to my brain again.

Marilyn had a good spirit. She was mellow, and one of the few people in the hospital who didn't cause me to get anxious. I decided that she was pretty good medicine.

So, these were the four people who consistently brought light to

A LITTLE HELP HERE...AND THERE

my day – Barbara, Maria the menu girl, Deana, and Marilyn. Also, when he had the occasion to make it to my room, Reggie was also cheery. It saddened me to know that my light bearers did not seem to include my neurologist, most of my team of doctors, most of my nurses and CNAs, and the hospital finance agents. I was surrounded by neutral entities and road blockers.

How did they expect me to get well? I began thinking that I would really have stop looking to other people, and to listen to myself, and my dream monkey guru, and not take heed to those around me who were doubtful or even neutral. Because if I followed the lead from those individuals, I was convinced that I would give up, accept the badge of the cripple, and probably never walk again.

11

GOOD NEWS FROM A DOCTOR?

Into my fourth week in the stroke wing of Saint Michael's, I was feeling pretty numb. I was getting stronger, yet had not gained any responsiveness on my right side. After a Sunday off, Marilyn the OT returned as part of my daily routine, along with Maria, the menu lady, Deana, the nurse and Barbara. My team was outclassed, but at least I had some dedicated players.

The fact that I was still at Saint Michael's after three weeks, without having the governor as a personal friend, was baffling everybody. Years later it would remain one of those puzzles lacking any reasonable explanation whatsoever. I speculated that the "powers that be," whoever they were, could apparently exercise certain privileges, and that the system had some camouflaged flexibility. But this notion did not solve the mystery of why or how I should find a place as benefactor.

I could only call myself fortunate. And if I'd believed in luck… Okay, I was pretty lucky. But I'd be contemplating the definition of that word for a long time.

GOOD NEWS FROM A DOCTOR?

Suddenly, Dr. Wendell came in, walking with a briskness that I had not witnessed before. And was that what it looked like? Was he actually smiling? NO! I couldn't believe my eyes! The dude was apparently having, for him, a "happy moment." I didn't think I would live to see the day when that stone face cracked.

"What's up, Doc'?" I said, figuring that the Warner Bros. star cartoon bunny comment might be acceptable humor, but it didn't appear that he'd caught the quip. The comic reference to the Warner Brothers rabbit, which was so iconic to children and adults worldwide, was lost to him.

"Well, we got you approved for Medi-Cal." His voice had only a trace of elevated tone which could be interpreted as cheeriness. Without seeing him, it could have passed as an accident of his usually neutral personality. But with the smile, that cinched it. Dr. Wendell was in a very rare visibly good mood.

"We're going to submit you for admission to a nursing facility that has better rehabilitation opportunities. You'll get more rehab time per day, and they'll have better equipment."

I was speechless. The kind of facility of which he spoke was only an option for people who had the best insurance or lots of money, and until he'd said that Medi-Cal had approved me, I'd had neither. I still didn't understand everything that Medi-Cal could do for me, but apparently, along with covering my hospital bills, it was my ticket into some kind of rehabilitation center, where I would continue to live as I had been in the hospital, and not be forced to go home to figure out how to survive.

I found my voice. "You're kidding! I thought Medi-Cal only took care of my hospital bills!"

"Yes, but under certain circumstances they'll help with extended care, acute rehab, and other things." I simply couldn't believe what

ROLAND'S STORY

I was hearing. Dr. Wendell continued. "And if we ask nice, they'll take care of your ongoing meds, a wheel chair, a walker, and other devices if you need them."

Then I got choked. My laugh seizure syndrome was engaged fully, only I wasn't laughing... I was crying. I had spent over three weeks practicing a "grin and bear it" role, not knowing how I would function if I was sent home, but knowing that it was inevitable.

I had just gotten strong enough to sit on the toilet without falling off. However, bending over for the cleanup still presented a problem. So far as I could figure, that was still a maneuver that would dethrone me. Now, the confronting of that, and many other issues, was postponed for a while.

Dr. Wendell hadn't witnessed my laugh seizures. But I guess he had seen enough stroke victims to know that I had what most of them had – a tendency towards emotional bursts with very little instigation. "It's okay, buddy. We're going to take care of you. You just hang in there." He patted me on my non-responsive arm as if to communicate a special message through it, turned, and headed for the door.

It appeared that my ragtag team had a quarterback after all, and we had just made a first down.

Goal to go!

PART II
Adventures in Rehab

12

REVIEW AND RELIEF

"They're sending me to a rehab in Lake Forest!" I exclaimed, incredulous at the news that I myself had only heard minutes before. "I'll be there for maybe a month!" Barbara's reaction was immediate, and expressed exactly what I was feeling.

"NO - WAY!" She spoke the words separately as though they were two statements. "I can't believe it!"

"Yes!" I confirmed. "They're going to transfer me this afternoon. The therapists tell me it's a great facility with a larger rehab workout area, with more equipment and advanced methodology." I couldn't wait to try everything.

It was Barbara's day off, which was unbelievably fortunate, for she'd be able to go with me, and we'd get acclimated to my new temporary residence together. She said she'd be with me at the hospital as soon as she could get there to pack up my things and prepare for the move.

When I ended the call, there was something final about that stage of my life phase. In just a few hours I would be back in an ambulance

ROLAND'S STORY

for another very expensive taxi ride, all on the medical coverage that I had believed was out of my reach. I'd be leaving Saint Michael's after an unprecedented four week and four day stay. No one - staff members, doctors, therapists – no one had ever heard of such an extended stay. Now I had some time to reflect, noting that, although some things did not seem like they were bearable, all things did indeed change, and nothing stayed the same. So they were endurable, and the key was not giving up.

I wasn't really obligated to take an accounting of my stay at Saint Michael's, but I started reviewing my incredible list of experiences that one wouldn't think could be likely from a hospital bed. I've taken the time to highlight the descriptions of the more important parts of my story. But there were numerous smaller issues, many of which were quite significant. Some of them are truly worth more than a mention, for as a mention, they're next to meaningless. Yet once described, one can appreciate the impact regarding their encounter.

One of the very first things I learned was how to pee in a plastic bottle while lying on my back. Sounds like the beginning of another joke, right? First of all, my bodily functions were not performing normally, and I was under constant fear of messing my bed, either from a late bed pan arrival, or a delayed urinal. For peeing, a man's perspective is usually standing, with legs spread, and guiding a stream into a trough or a toilet - a rather large target with a device that had aiming ability.

My strategies for the simple task of relieving myself had changed pretty radically. I couldn't stand. That left lying on my side, or lying on my back. Lying on my back trumped the other option, because I couldn't add the effort of trying to balance on my side while I exposed myself and endeavored to guide myself into a three inch wide hole while juggling the container. Definitely not the most comfortable position in which to relax. Plus, the urinals were smooth and almost weightless.

For a critical item such as it was, one had to wonder whose idea it was to make them so light, slippery, and oddly cumbersome and hard to grasp. It would take me at least two months to be secure with urinal handling. It's quite odd to know that you're the master of a noteworthy accomplishment requiring so much personal experience, when your initiation to the subject is abrupt, and you're handed the item devoid of introduction or explanation. And the establishment had no certifications for proper and safe urinal use, no matter how much of an expert you became.

So, my new method of relieving myself required quite an adjustment, which, having no time to think about it, became one of the first of my many temporary, long term, changes in operations. And, of course I got a lot of practice. I needed to keep an empty urinal close at hand, either hanging by its handle on the bed rail, or positioned on the bed table, often next to my water bottle.

As absurd as it sounds, those two objects became table partners out of necessity. To hang it on the bed rail was a disaster waiting to happen. In a hurry, it was bound to get hung up and stuck on the rail. And there was the likelihood that it would remain there when I decided to sit in a chair, which was invariably on the opposite side of the bed. In any case of urgency, it was just bad news. And relieving oneself was always a case of urgency. Otherwise, the idea never came to mind. For me in a hospital bed, it wasn't a matter of how soon or how far until the next public toilet. The time line was always now. My toilet was in arm's reach, any time I wanted it. At least, it was supposed to be within reach.

Often the nurses would rearrange things to conduct some

periodic tests, or the daily bed changing crew would clear things in order to give me clean sheets and pillow cases. At times the therapists would set me up to transfer to a chair, and I would end up there after therapy was complete, as opposed to the bed. In these cases, any person involved could relocate my urinal, or inadvertently leave me out of its reach. The clincher was when whoever was responsible also left me out of reach of my remote that they had provided me in order to contact a nurse, which also controlled the TV. Then, in one short visit, I could be left recovering from a therapy workout, having to pee with no urinal, stuck watching a sitcom with the sound off, with no way to summon help except to holler. I got better at disregarding my physical effect of fatigue in order to keep my wits, and run the mental checklist of hazards from visitors and staff before they left the room.

It was important to find a way to hold the urinal steady, and not let it slip from its position while in use. Getting it into position quickly was a necessary skill. Rushing to do this could cause the losing of control and maybe dropping the urinal on the floor, possibly resulting in disaster. Once the process of relief was complete, there was still a cleanup to follow.

I recall an old saying regarding this subject: "No matter how much you shake it, the last drop always lands in your shorts." Well, I hadn't been wearing any underwear since my stay in the hospital began. The backless medical gown was my new standard. But regardless, there was the issue of "the last drop." I developed a technique involving a tissue that became indispensable in keeping me and my gown dry. Still, there were occasionally minor accidents that required new bedsheets or garment changes, or both.

Lastly, there was the capping of the lid that was attached to the handle to close the container. Done. Who would have ever guessed

REVIEW AND RELIEF

that one would have to develop such skills at age fifty-eight? And inevitably, the urinal took its proper place next to my water bottle, in spite of the obvious unease of nurses, CNAs, and visitors. Although there was an element of repulsion, for me it was all about convenience. These were two things that I just needed to keep handy at all times.

After I'd finished my job of relieving myself, there was still the need to summon a CNA or a nurse to dump the urinal and prepare it for its next use. I admired their diligence to perform this task without hesitation or attitude. Under any other circumstances a request of, "Would you mind dumping this out and rinsing the container?" would be to solicit a response like, "Do it yourself, you jerk!" Yet the nurses and their assistants performed this task as willingly as checking your pulse, and quite a bit more often. My respect for them grew.

Daily meals presented more things to conquer. There was the issue of cheap plastic utensils. There were also creamer capsules, jelly serving portions, salad dressings in sealed pouches, jello cups, pudding cups, sugar substitutes, mini-tubs of fake butter, milk cartons, and even lids on coffee cups that were meant to keep the coffee warm as opposed to keep me from drinking it – all of which added to the challenges of consuming my daily meals.

Plastic wrap was among the cruelest of jokes. In use, it wasn't a process of industrial packaging, made to be user friendly. Someone went out of their way to take something made in the facility kitchen and render it almost unattainable by wrapping the clingiest plastic that could be found around the glass container, sealing in freshness, preventing spillage, and for me, transforming a part of my meal into a physics problem and a brain teaser.

Among the most difficult things to learn was how to cut food with the plastic knife. Eating with marginal plastic forks and spoons was difficult enough. But the meals often came with the food virtually inedible, unless I could cut it into smaller bites. Turkey in gravy wasn't something I could easily pick up and eat with my fingers. Nor were pork chops in a sauce. Ham slices were definitely in the problem category. But probably the dirtiest trick of all was to place several thick slices of tasty roast beef in front of me that were overcooked just enough to resist any maneuver to produce bite-sized pieces, except sawing with that silly, serrated, plastic knife.

The thing was, I knew that the knife was totally capable of dividing and conquering that beef if I could just find a way to keep it from moving around. The designers had cleverly engineered an implement that, with five or six slides across whatever food substance you chose, was capable of efficiently slicing through it. The real riddle was how to get the meat to hold still.

Upon my first attempt, I realized that I had to approach the problem from a higher intellectual perspective. My caveman instincts caused me to hack with the serrated knife so that the meat remained unaffected, but the primitive lashing motion grabbed the chunk of beef and shoved it around, causing everything else on the plate to scatter, resulting in vegies and mashed potatoes to relocate to the tray, the table, and me. Hence, the bib.

At this point, I was well aware that I was going to have to outwit my circumstances. The immediate issue was to not get so excited about my food so as to get careless. It became obvious that, with only one hand and no assist, the knife was not going to function as it was originally designed. It was an implement of co-dependence when what I needed was a tool of independence. In the end, my conclusion was that I had to find a new way of using an old tool.

I tried several things. No matter what I did, the meat could not be counted on to cooperate with the normal slicing activity. After

REVIEW AND RELIEF

many tries, I did notice that simply putting significant pressure on the meat with my knife would compress it and leave an indentation. I theorized that if I did that enough times I was bound to be successful in cutting through. It was the controlled brute force technique.

What I needed to know was that it was possible, and I eventually proved my theory. But I also concluded, after several minutes of hard work, that by the time I had reduced the object of my aggression to a consumable condition, the product of my efforts may not be enough to sustain me... I'd probably starve of malnutrition. I surely was burning more calories than the meat had to offer in return. So, I had to find a way to be more efficient.

During the course of a few weeks, I eventually developed the best cutting procedure. It was a combination of rocking with the curve of the blade, twisting length-wise, using the knife near its tip to chip away at the cut a quarter of an inch at a time, then adding a coup de grace blow that separated the meat into new chunks, sliding the pieces apart. If this last move was not performed the results could be a nuisance.

For instance, if I switched to the spoon to pick up the piece of meat, and I had not completed the cut, the target piece would start to rise from the plate just enough to reveal that it was still attached by thin piece of sinew that was just strong enough to pull the piece off my spoon and redeposit it back to my plate, usually in a splash of gravy. However, if I chose the fork, I would spend a concentrated couple of seconds effectively stabbing the bite to make sure it could successfully make the journey to my mouth, only to find that it came with another, sometimes quite large, piece of meat also attached. I could employ additional tactics, such as shaking it, spinning the fork, or dragging the trailing chunk across my plate, hoping it would let go of my bite, and sometimes it would. But any of those maneuvers had their own contingencies, such as meat falling into gravy, more food displaced from my plate, or the snap of severing meat strands sending flicks of sauce in all directions.

In the end, I learned patience in making sure that each piece was cut completely. I extended that patience to include waiting until all the meat was rendered bite sized before I began eating. That way, once I started eating I could continue without interrupting my moments of enjoyment with repeated segments of challenge and frustration. It was a perfect display of delayed gratification. This refinement of meal processing became something of an ordeal. But spending the time doing it kept me from hating meals and focusing on the things I thought I couldn't do, robbing me of more of life's simple enjoyments, like eating a good bite of roast beef.

One of the earliest recovery challenges was to sit up by myself. The PT's goal was initially to get me sitting upright without toppling over on my right side. It took me most of my stay at Saint Michael's to regain only seventy-five percent of this skill. At the same time, I had a more critical, yet connected goal – sitting up by myself on the toilet. To be able to do this stunt with my new physical limitations was the equivalent of learning how to do a back flip on a trampoline... which I never mastered. I practiced training my left side muscles to compensate for my weakened right side, and adjusted the position of my left leg to the center line of my body in order to support all of my weight.

It was all of three weeks before I made it to the point of moderate stability, so that if I concentrated, I could keep myself from falling off my pedestal. I was able to handle it, but I had to fake my confidence so that the nurses and CNAs would think I was good to go, and leave me by myself for a few minutes. That still left me with a final stage to attend to. I wasn't yet coordinated enough to

REVIEW AND RELIEF

lean forward and support the weight shift in order to perform a final cleaning.

Until I was able to do this, I was helpless to wipe myself, and had to bite the proverbial bullet, subjecting myself to the pre-toddler condition of needing to call for help. In order not to feel demoralized, I was obliged to graciously accept the kind help of nurses and assistants, male and female alike, knowing that I would eventually reclaim my faltering dignity.

There were things that were to be ongoing hassles for months. There were conditions related to upper body, diaphragmatic, and abdominal muscle and nerve damage. Whatever parts were affected on the right half of my body, they in turn affected my breathing, digestion, and central body strength. Other than my arm and leg, there were muscles from my right shoulder to my right butt cheek that were flaccid or greatly weakened. The resulting effects included the inability to cough on purpose and clear my throat, do even a poor imitation of a situp, and perform a task as simple as blowing my nose.

Occasionally, mucous would gather in my throat, and my vocal chords would suddenly not perform as they should. My words would either come out soft and fuzzy, or accompanied by harsh gurgling sounds that rendered my attempt at conversation useless. Sometimes my voice would only function at half volume and clarity for an extended several hours. Sometimes I experienced a roller coaster of conditions, clear, then clogged, repeating throughout day.

Although I wasn't necessarily tired, there were times that I would yawn every few minutes. And not just two or three yawns in a row. It was more like twenty or thirty yawns in a row, and I use those numerical examples only because I failed to keep an accurate count. A yawn can feel good. It can be relaxing, adding a good

ROLAND'S STORY

stretch. A yawn is usually accompanied by a great inhale, feeding your lungs and body with much needed oxygen. But yawns also paused your mental processing while this was going on. And after a good number of yawns, even if I wasn't tired to start with, I was left with a relaxed body, a blank mind, and an abolished sense of motivation and purpose. So even when I wasn't technically sleepy, there were times when I would yawn incessantly. I couldn't watch a TV show and expect to follow what was going on. Completing an email was a problem when I had the yawns. I surmised that my weakened body was not getting enough oxygen, and sometimes taking some deep breaths would help.

I've never been prone to hiccups. Now, an hour would not pass without a few hiccups interrupting whatever I was doing – talking, therapy workout, eating... anything but sleeping. They were fairly severe in nature, as hiccups tend to be. But these also tended to be joined by an occasional burp, the kind that introduced stomach acid to the action and caused burning in the throat, interrupting normal breathing for several minutes.

What caused hiccups anyway? When I researched this question several sources offered clues. Eating too much... no. Drinking too much alcohol... not even, since I didn't drink alcohol. Swallowing too much air... oooookay... Smoking... nope, didn't smoke. Sudden changes in temperature, such as a hot drink followed immediately by a cold drink... maybe. But by the time most hot drinks got to me in the hospital bed they were usually lukewarm. Emotional stress or excitement... well, maybe during the first couple of days. But otherwise, no. Being in the hospital, I was somewhat anxiety prone from impatience. But I wouldn't have called it stressful... not exactly.

Maybe if I had been waiting for the doctor to offer a verdict on

REVIEW AND RELIEF

cancer tests, or other disease analysis, I would have been stressed out. But I had already been handed my prognosis, and at least I wasn't having a life threatening emergency anymore. Being a patient was a notoriously boring, tedious, and uneventful existence, for the most part. If it hadn't been for my laptop, I would have gone nuts. Although hiccups did not fit the classifications of interesting, entertaining, or enlightening, they definitely were not boring. I'm not sure that I'd call that a plus. I'd have to think about that one.

I've given it some thought, and decided that hiccups were definitely an annoying hazard and a nuisance. What touched me every time they occurred was that I had no explanation, from the hospital staff or Wikipedia, what had caused them. No suggested explanation made any sense. Funny how such a seemingly simple and common problem escaped the conglomerate intelligence of the entire medical industry, plus the collective experience of worldwide bloggers. I just wanted to understand why I had been chosen to have this affliction.

After a young man reaches puberty, most of the questions concerning his manhood were answered by applying the stimulus of Playboy magazines and a flashlight under the sheets. But there were a few distinct moments later in life when a man must wonder about his spontaneous manliness. One of those times was in the days immediately following a vasectomy. Another was after a stroke.

It's easy to understand why the subject of a vasectomy would be worried. Usually this was a father, conscientiously submitting to a minor outpatient surgical procedure, insuring against the possibilities of personally contributing to the unnecessary increasing population of the world, and of course the size of his family. However, his intentions never included sacrificing the obvious pleasures attached to the ownership of certain private parts. After some brief, and probably furious, desperate experimentation, he'd be relieved

ROLAND'S STORY

to find that everything worked quite well, in spite of the wielding of the fatal blade.

Having a stroke was different. Down the middle of my body was an imaginary line that was not perfectly drawn, and half of my body functioned quite well, while the other half had serious malfunctions. I could only guess which half of me held motor authority to the parts in question. This was serious. I began imagining how I was going to feel if the half of my body that was playing hooky included the private appendage of which I had only one.

When using the urinal, that minor bit of manipulation resulted in nothing telling. In considering that mood was always a factor, trying to keep from wetting the bed or my gown was not exactly inspiring. Occasionally I experimented, but felt too conspicuous to get serious. Being in a room with a camera continuously aimed at me was also demotivating. I could just imagine one or several nurses or CNAs standing over the playback monitors and snickering. I couldn't bring myself to pursue the answer to the question in earnest.

One evening I dosed off into a deep sleep as a late night classic lost my attention. The volume was low, the movie a non-contrasting black and white, and the plot less than captivating. I may have gone channel surfing looking for something of interest. I guess I wasn't too successful, and eventually was caught by a wave of slumber. When I came awake it was in the wee hours. It was probably after two A.M. Most of the hospital must have been asleep. The room was dark except a bit of light coming from the TV on the wall. The vision on the screen was near motionless, and the shot was a close-up, so that as my vision cleared I could gradually make out a voluptuously curved female breast, not so discretely covered in red lace. The camera slowly progressed down her bare stomach to

REVIEW AND RELIEF

reveal a red garter attached to red stockings, the motion carefully traveling in order to suggest and not show.

I stared in awe, wondering how a hospital TV station could offer such visions. I knew it couldn't be a pay-per-view concept. Wait a minute – hadn't I been watching a black and white oldie? Oh, well... I may have changed stations. Just then a seductive voice spoke, obvious not belonging to the female on the screen. "Call me..." it echoed as the slow motion camera continued to display the vixen in red from assorted angles. "I'm here waiting for you!"

As I finally became fully conscious I realized that I was watching a commercial. It was devised to entice the curious male into calling a number and giving up a credit card with approval to be charged several dollars per minute to have a live, invisible woman speak seductively to the caller while dressed in a worn out bathrobe, hair in curlers, sleeping child in a sling hanging from a shoulder, and ironing her waitresses apron that she would wear to work the next day.

The vision tickled me, and I smiled, almost falling prey to a laugh spasm. As I managed to avoid the seizure, I was aware that the video was actually well-produced and of high quality. Captivated, the thought crossed my mind that the producers of the video were people who really knew their jobs. I could just imagine some lonely guy, lacking flirting skills, gladly putting up some money to have a fantasy date with a voice that sounded like it could belong to the girl on TV. Actually, she looked very hot. It was pretty easy to imagine what she would be like... warm and soft... willing...

Nothing in the room had moved. My body was still in its most common position, on my back, right arm on a pillow, only my gown covering me. Inspecting my motionless body, I was in for a shock. Below my waist, my gown rose several inches higher than normal, and I realized that I was actually aroused.

ROLAND'S STORY

What! Seriously? I reached down with my left hand to check my theory. There was my solo private part enjoying a happy moment.

My relief was tremendous. If I hadn't caught myself, my exclamations could have brought the nurse into this scene with me caught in a pickle after swinging my bat at the pitch, and "Miss Let's Play Ball!" on TV, alluringly trapping me between first and second base.

"Yes!" I said to myself quietly, and remembering the camera, I let go of myself.

Then the whole comical element finally overwhelmed me, and I gave in to the laugh seizure that was inevitable, knowing that this was one funny joke that was going to be as hard to deliver as naming a brown chariot rider.

13

A NEW REHAB AND THE KILLER FOG

It was after four o'clock by the time the ambulance/taxi arrived at the hospital. Barbara had gotten there with hours to spare, so I was packed and ready by noon. This allowed us to share one last less-than-memorable meal from the hospital cafe, and relax the few hours until it was time to go.

We sat marveling at the overall event of a thirty-three day hospital stay. I doubted that the booking of a penthouse suite at the Bellagio in Las Vegas was as expensive. It was mind boggling. It was altogether possible that my bill already exceeded what Barbara and I made in a year. The conversation reviewed the doctors, the nurses, and the therapists. With the exceptions of my PT, Marilyn, and a few wonderful nurses, I was left without anything resembling remorse at the thought of leaving.

During my stay at Saint Michael's, I had fended off most requests by friends to come see me. I didn't feel all that presentable. Nor was

ROLAND'S STORY

I actually in need of moral support or a pep talk. Yet my best friend, Diran, could not be denied. He had taken it upon himself to confirm whether or not I could have visitors, checked the available times, and just showed up bearing gifts... the edible kind.

We had made a tradition of going to a Persian restaurant once in a while, and have an incredible lunch that was surprisingly healthy. Knowing why I was in the hospital, and double-checking to make sure that the food still fit the standards of acceptable consumption, he elected to bring me the lunch that I always ate, packaged to go, from the Persian restaurant, and gave me a weekly highlight to an otherwise boring existence, with the exception of Barbara's daily vigil, and my collection of odd medical center events.

In spite of Barbara's daily efforts, a couple of visitors, and the dedication of Diran, it was difficult to break out of the syndrome of dullness. I was used to playing racquetball three times a week, driving to networking meetings, meeting clients and friends for coffee, and more. My life had shriveled to a range of fifteen feet from my bed, with rare exceptions, such as an occasional wheelchair ride to a concrete smoker's patio to get a few minutes of sun.

Stir crazy was one way to describe what I felt. Anxious for a change of scenery? Yes. Ready for some inspiration? Indeed! I really wanted someone in attendance to act like I was going to get well, or at least believe that I had a chance for improvement. I came to the conclusion that there were some serious problems regarding the medical industry as a whole to generate the monetary exchange that it did, cash, insurance or otherwise, and yet be so lacking in emotional support and encouragement. So, in relocating, I had high expectations that an official rehabilitation center would have something much greater to offer, and that there would be more value for the investment. At this point, it wasn't my money, thank God. But

A NEW REHAB AND THE KILLER FOG

it seemed that there was an incredible waste and inefficiency, along with a general lack of enthusiasm for healing.

Barbara had made multiple trips to her car, taking all the things that I had accumulated during the course of a month. In an effort to cheer me up and on, she had spent a lot of her time while at work and driving thinking up ways to put a smile on my face. It made sense, when taking into consideration how much weight the authorities would place on the will to live as being a factor in whether a critical patient lived or died, that they would regard a patient's attitude to be important in healing at all levels.

My attitude was definitely not lacking. I wanted to be a part of a miraculous plot. Something leaning towards unbelievable suited me just fine. I knew my critical stage of danger was over. But I still wanted to be impressed with my own state of mind and my own efforts, and with the magical unseen and unknown that could influence my recovery. I didn't need my bed to glow in the dark, or an act of the supernatural that the religious minded would call a spiritual event and others would call a fluke of natural physics. It was okay if they couldn't tell me why I got better, and I didn't want my name in the papers. I just wanted to take full advantage of any and all opportunities.

My willingness to take all comers was inclusive of the deliverance of a prayer from a volunteer making the rounds to lift spirits one afternoon, accompanied by a full three verses in well-sung acapella of "Amazing Grace." I wasn't sure if I benefited more from her visit, or she did. Her dual personification of a cheerful, sweet angel, and at the same time a forlorn, conquered soul was quite a contradiction.

I let her have a few moments, and genuinely appreciated her efforts. She finished with a bit of prayer, and a declaration of faith. Her lips showed a smile, but her eyes could not mask her tortured

ROLAND'S STORY

soul. I thanked her, and as she left the room, I sincerely hoped that our time together had helped ease her pain. Although I didn't think seriously for a second that I'd rise from my bed and walk as a result of her heartfelt ministrations, I did conclude there were a select few people who did all that they could do to make things better. Not necessarily for exorbitantly inflated fees charged for work delivered like a blue collar industry, lacking in individual commitment to excellence or personal involvement. This did not pertain to all staff members. But I was disturbed to note that it was the majority to which this description applied.

It so happened that Deana was on duty that day. She had cheered with me when she heard the news, truly happy for my opportunity to achieve the next stage of therapy. She spent an extra thirty minutes late that morning telling what she knew of Lynfield Rehab Center and Nursing Home. I gathered from her comments that the facility was the rehab of choice, and it was fortunate for Barbara and me that it was located next to our home town. It apparently was an outstanding place to go to for stroke recovery, with two work out rooms, electronic stimulation machines, and lots of therapists to apply me to new challenges.

My goodbyes were few and brief. As it was, on any given day, I would commonly see maybe eight people other than Barbara – two nurses, two CNAs, a PT, an OT, the food deliverer, and the doctor on duty, if he didn't drop by while I was napping. When the ambulance crew of two arrived, there was the nurse, Deana, and her CNA. The therapists had come in the early afternoon, so there was little fanfare, and I was fine with that. None of this had been a party. I guess I was most affected by the thought of no longer having Marilyn as my OT, and hoped that I could have a therapist assigned to me at the new facility who was as caring, and as skilled.

A NEW REHAB AND THE KILLER FOG

There were a few faces to wave at, and people, many of whom had heard of me and my long extended stay, watching as I left like I was some kind of unusual, rare breed of patient. I had wanted to say goodbye to Dr. Wendell, that odd man who had hidden behind a grimace of a mask, who had turned out to be the fourth quarter hero and MVP of the Saint Michael's game. But he wasn't anywhere near when the time came, and I hadn't thought to request an audience with him. I was relieved in a way, because sentimentality made me a little teary-eyed under normal circumstances. I was afraid that anything more touching, like thanking my doc' for actions and bravery above and beyond the call of duty, especially under my present condition, would cause me to cry like a little girl.

The crew rolled me out to the loading dock, put me into the ambulance, and we were off to get on the freeway, down three exits, and off again, cruising a familiar thoroughfare leading to my next stop. It seemed odd that I was actually in my own "stomping grounds," yet inside the hospital it had felt like a foreign country. The very same was to be true of my new facility. Once inside, there was nothing familiar for me to relate to, and nothing to connect me to my pre-stroke life. I felt like I was isolated from everything. The ride to the rehab center merely felt like a teaser to show me a quick and limited glimpse of the world from which I had been abruptly kidnapped over a month before.

When we arrived at Lynfield Rehab Center and Nursing Home there was the distinct impression of entering a senior citizens home. Although some patients were as young as late forties or fifties, the vast majority appeared to be of retirement age or older. Wheelchairs were everywhere, and most of them were occupied. During my stay at Lynfield, I was to witness only two patients who were not in wheelchairs for their primary mode of mobility, and those two were in walkers.

I was outside the ambulance for a brief few seconds as I was

ROLAND'S STORY

rolled to the front door, during which time I saw what looked like a one-story building with stucco walls and a Spanish tile roof. At least it more resembled a motel than a hospital. There the image of vacation hospitality faded as the paramedics wheeled me through the entrance, past the front desk, and down a series of halls lined with doorways to rooms that could have passed for those in a motel, were it not for the sterile-looking accommodations obviously designed for practicality and utility. Each room came equipped with two identical mechanically powered twin beds, two TVs, two dressers, linoleum floors, and the smell of mild disinfectant cleaner in the air.

I was one of the younger patients in my section. The few others who were my age or younger were spread around the one-hundred-and-thirty bed facility so that some of them I never met. But it was good to meet anybody at this point, and I was willing to talk to anyone. When I learned that I would have a roommate, I was both excited and concerned. It meant that I would forfeit the privacy of having my own room. However, I was open to having companionship.

On the way to my room, I was able to catch a glimpse of the locals. Some were little old ladies and men who looked like they were poured into their seats. I had to wonder how these people could exist in their limp, twisted conditions. I couldn't imagine the process of transferring them from bed to wheelchair, and back again. Then again, many were so depleted and fragile that one nurse or CNA could probably pick them up and move them in one fell swoop. But sometimes their fragility was such that extra care was needed so that a simple move didn't break brittle bones or dislocate joints. Even if bones and joints were still fairly healthy, muscles could be atrophied or torn from diseases or accidents.

It became apparent to me that all my fellow residents were not necessarily there to completely rehabilitate. After a brief view I realized that the "nursing home" part of the facility housed many people who were spending the rest of their lives being cared for with no intention of improving their conditions. The best example of this was my new roommate, Willy. I was to meet him after dinner.

Meanwhile, the paramedics finished their jobs efficiently, transferring me to the bed closest to the door. Barbara was minutes behind, her arms laden with the accoutrements that would establish my comfort zone in the new facility – t-shirts, laptop, sugar-free treats, and regular sweetened treats to bribe and sway staff members to enhance my stay in their care.

An aid that reminded me of a typical hospital "candy striper" came in, except that she had no candy stripes. She did have a lanyard around her neck, and a rectangular I.D. with her picture that told me that she was indeed a representative of the facility. However, my hunch was right. She spoke with a child-like squeak that told us that she was maybe sixteen years old, and couldn't be part of their regular staff.

"Hi, my name is Tina, and I'm here to tell you welcome to Lynfield Rehab Center and Nursing Home, we hope you have a pleasant stay, and if you need anything please let us know, and the nurse will be with you as soon as she can, and if you haven't had dinner just tell the nurse and she'll make sure they send you a meal, and thank you for letting us serve." She headed for the door without waiting for any acknowledgment or reaction of any kind. Her speech had been delivered with the consistency of a middle school science lab project analysis, and with as much personality that would probably have been required to get a passing grade.

I said to her as she made her exit, "Thanks, Tina!" And she was gone without looking back.

Barbara said, "That was odd..." But now she was thinking. "You

ROLAND'S STORY

know, maybe I'll step out to that Chinese food place that's right over there, and get us something to split, just in case the default meal isn't worth eating." She was pointing like we could see through the walls, but I was so turned around from the gurney trip, and making too many left turns to count, that I could only guess at the possible target.

"Heheheh! And if it is worth eating, we can mix and match and both sample the local fare!" I was in a decent mood, even with the colorful initiation we had, and was happy being in a new place promising new experiences. Barb kissed me and said that she'd be back in a bit.

Shortly thereafter, staff members started checking in with me to welcome me and place themselves at my disposal. It was definitely more relaxed than the hospital. I began believing that my life was about to brighten. A nurse came in for a brief hello named Kendra. Also, a tall, more casually dressed lady came in, and I got the idea that she wasn't of the nursing clan. She stood with a clipboard held with one arm pressed against her left side and a pen in her right hand. Attaching the pen to her clipboard, she extended her open hand to me.

"Stacy, Mr. Takaoka." She said, and offered me a genuine smile. "I'm your case manager."

"Hi, Stacy, and it's Roland." I smiled back at her as I offered her my left hand inverted. She took my hand firmly and held it longer than I expected, and we became immediate friends.

"Just wanted to welcome you to Lynfield." She held my returned gaze with warm eyes, and I knew the smile was not canned. She acted as if I were telling one of my jokes and had not yet gotten to the punch line. If she only knew. This lady liked her job. "I'll be watching over you as your case worker during your stay, and if you need anything, you can have me summoned, because I work here in

A NEW REHAB AND THE KILLER FOG

the front office. I'm here basically every day until five or six, except weekends. And when I'm not here, there's always someone in our office during the day to respond."

"Stacy, you will probably hardly ever hear from me." I said. "I doubt that there will be any issues. But initially I might have a few questions."

"Sure. Any time. It's late today, so the doctor won't be seeing you until tomorrow sometime. Also, the therapists will check in with you and do an initial assessment, after which time they will start you on a daily program." I knew this was going to be another period of "getting to know me," by the therapists as they figured out what I could and could not do.

"Well, you just answered all of my questions! If I think of anything else I'll let you know." And then I added, "I'm bound to think of something. I tend to be pretty curious."

"Not a problem." She was a person of positive vibes. I felt that she would be someone that I could get straight answers from. "Can I get you anything now?"

"No, I'm good, thanks. My wife will here in a few minutes, and we're going to have dinner." I mainly wanted to get comfortable, and settle in for the night. "I would like to know if you have wifi here, and whether I need a pass code."

Stacy answered, "Yeah, I'll look into that for you. I know we have wireless Internet. Is there anything else?"

"Thanks, but that's all I can think of for now, except... I was wondering about dinner?" We had covered everything on my mind for the time being.

"Yes! Tonight we can fix you up with something. They always prepare extra food. Tomorrow you will be picking from a set menu. You also have a selection of options, like a chef salad, a fruit plate, a hamburger, and a few things. I'll get a copy of the list and post it on your wall. The regular menu is monthly, and I'll find you a copy of that."

"You are actually going to feed me a hamburger? With chips or fries?" Being type 2 diabetic and in rehab for a stroke, this was a bit startling.

"Let's see..." She was looking at pages on her clipboard. "Yes, you appear to be on a standard diet, with solids, low sodium. So, they may go easy on the chips with you."

"That's amazing." I said, wondering if they were going to surprise me by adding packets of catsup.

We wrapped up the conversation with small talk, and Stacy left, promising to follow up on menus and wifi. I liked her. I had a feeling that my new team was already forming.

Now, expecting dinner from two directions, I had time to examine my surroundings. In my new bed, I was elevated at the knees and inclined nearly to a sitting position. Pretty comfortable bed, overall. Whereas the previous hospital bed was designed with special padding down the sides, I guess to keep a body towards the center and less likely to roll off the bed, this one was perfectly flat. The hospital bed was inflatable, and the therapists had used that feature when trying to balance me sitting on the side of the bed.

It was much easier to sit on the inflated bed. When not inflated, I had a hard time achieving the sitting position at all, let alone sitting without assistance for any length of time. This bed was uniformly flat, other than when the back was inclined or the knee section raised. Additionally, the whole framework for the bed raised and lowered. I had visions of tall nurses to short nurses all trying to efficiently do their jobs. I was to discover that it wasn't the nurses' height that determined the bed elevation, but the technique being performed on the patient that required the height adjustment.

A NEW REHAB AND THE KILLER FOG

Beyond the generic but very practical bed, the room was a throwback to "eighties budget modern." The dressers and a chair were the only pieces of furniture except for a bed table like the one I got to know so well at Saint Michael's. The dressers were distinctly different from each other, and looked like they were two choice second hand pieces from the Salvation Army. The chair, likewise, had the eighties utilitarian look that was not quite built for comfort, and significantly missed the mark for style. Between the two beds, and circling so as to enclose the patient and block sight from the front door, was an efficient system of curtains that, when drawn, could separate the beds, and hide either or both from public view. It wasn't sound proof, but it was fairly private. It took me all of two minutes to measure what was now my new temporary home, and I figured that it was livable. Considering that my objective was to heal, after a few weeks I might just decide that it was time to stand up and walk out of that colorless environment. Maybe that was a part of therapy.

It was nearing the end of the dinner hour, and I was just starting to get bored. The walls hadn't changed, no one else was coming in to check on the new guy, and I wasn't set up yet with laptop and Internet. But the sideshow was about to begin. And that is not a statement meant to poke fun or degrade. What was about to happen was genuinely entertaining.

I heard a rumbling of rubber wheels, and the rattle of plastic. The sounds came from a large structure that was designed out of two inch PVC pipe, and vaguely resembled a box without sides or top. As it rolled slowly into my room, it transformed, first into a three dimensional frame, then a chair. I recognized that what I was viewing was a custom built walker that served as a standing walker, a sitting sled, and a protective shield against walls, doorways, and any obstacles in the path.

ROLAND'S STORY

In the seat, which was just a square piece of plywood covered with a large cushion secured in place with tie downs, was a gigantic man. He wasn't fat. He was just tall. In his day the coach would have insisted that he try out for JV basketball whether he had ever touched one or not. Without unfolding him to be measured, he had to be at least six-feet-seven-or-eight inches tall. This was stunning, because if people actually did shrink when they got older, this man wasn't going to be a good example. My first overall impression was that I was looking at a Frankenstein. The analogy was completely ill-placed. Unlike the image of a gargantuan countenance in shredded clothing, and a scary face with stitch marks, my new roomie was tall, yes, but otherwise as docile-looking as a teddy bear. He was dressed in pajama bottoms with a drawstring waist, t-shirt covered by a red cardigan sweater, tennies, and a baseball cap. Rather than Frankenstein, what appeared before me was a bigger-than-life-size, senior citizen version of Howdy Doody.

Arturo, the CNA, was the motor for the PVC carriage, and he nodded when he followed the walker into the room and saw me occupying the first bed.

"Hola!" Arturo said cheerfully, assuming that I would understand such common Spanish.

"Hola! Como estas?" I said in return. And Arturo was obviously pleased, and went into a string of Spanish that totally lost me after, "Mui bien, gracias! dada, dada, da dada..." Obviously he was under the impression that I was prepared and equipped to carry on this mode of conversation. He saw me shaking my head, and realized that he'd lost me. "Oh... hehe... your Spanish not too good?"

"No. Not too good. I fake it." And Arturo cracked up laughing. Just then the man riding in the PVC carriage turned his head in my direction, and appeared to stare right at me.

A NEW REHAB AND THE KILLER FOG

"What's your name?" Arturo asked.

"Roland." I replied.

"Who's that?" Willy asked, with a blank look on his face. Although it looked like he could see me, actually he could only see shadows and vague outlines.

"That's your new roommate, Mr. Willy. His name is Roland." Arturo spoke loudly with an emphasis on articulation.

"Hi, Willy!" I said.

Willy continued looking at me as if I were from another planet. But although his face was almost expressionless, his voice showed a wealth of personality. "Hello!"

"How are you doing today?" I tried to speak clearly, in spite of my lazy lip and tendency to slur words.

"I'm fine." Willy replied, just as cheery as he could be. He followed right along with, "And how are YOU doing?" Delivered by anyone else, his question may have been interpreted as sarcastic. But he was just exchanging pleasant conversation, and doing the polite thing in redirecting the subject off of himself and on to me.

"I'm doing great, Willy. Thanks." I said. It seemed to be the end of the exchange.

Arturo rambled on, mostly as an accompaniment to his coaxing Willy from the PVC carriage to his bed, and mixing meaningless empty phrases like, "Yeah, we're all fine today..." and, "...okay, stand up, Mr. Willy... stand up, okay..." Arturo got Willy into bed, and spent the next few minutes removing his shoes and red cardigan.

"Yeah, Mr. Willy is a hero!" Offered Arturo. "He was in World War II." He added.

At which point Willy caught his cue, and began to sing. "From the halls of Montezuma, to the shores of Tripoli..." He was not bad. "... we will fight our country's battles on the land and on the sea."

ROLAND'S STORY

I pictured the ranks of soldiers that Willy evidently imagined himself standing with, and wondered if he saw himself as a part of a choir or singing a solo.

"If the Army and the Navy... and the ...hmmm hmmm..." He obviously was having trouble with the second part of the verse. But as I listened, I realized he was singing words that I had never heard. If the Army and the Navy, whatever? That wasn't how the song went. I remembered, "The Marine's Hymn" well. "First to fight for right and freedom, and to keep our honor clean..." Yeah, that was how it was supposed to go. But Willy continued on, and I supposed that at some point in his gradual fade from reality he had decided that his made up words were the real ones. "Hmm hmm uh huh. dada... title, the United States Marines." He certainly ended with flourish, and I almost expected him to salute the ceiling.

I was touched by this man's spirit. I was to find that the entire staff knew him, and called him, "Mr. Willy." Willis Weatherby was indeed a World War II veteran, and apparently something of a recognized war hero. He was as nice an old guy as they came, a gentleman, still congenial, polite, and complimentary, even though he was ninety-one years old, mostly blind and suffering from advanced stages of dementia. He slept from seven-thirty or eight in the evening until six A.M. when they woke him each day to prepare him for breakfast. By one-thirty they would transfer him back to bed to nap for a couple of hours. Then they would get him back up to have dinner, and wait an hour or two, when they would help him into bed for the night. Willy was to prove to be an almost perfect roommate, with no complaints coming from his side of the room, and hardly any noise. There were, however, going to be a few unavoidable contingencies.

Barbara walked in carrying a plastic bag that held the Chinese food, and I was suddenly very grateful to have her in my life. It wasn't the food, but what it represented. It stood for that additional bit of comfort and benefit that would not have been there. Throughout the ordeal she had been positive and supportive, never missing a day to come visit me, even if she worked until 10:30 at night. She was always thinking of something that could make my life a little more enjoyable under the circumstances, and going as far out of her way as necessary to make it happen.

This became a vivid issue as I got to know my roomie. Willy was old, and had apparently outlived the rest of any family that was nearby enough to visit regularly. In the weeks that I would spend at Lynfield, I was to see not one visitor for Wally. I guess the Lynfield staff was his family. That meant that anything out of the ordinary, or routine, for a nursing home to highlight Willy's day was going to have to come from a staff member's good will. Thankfully, I had someone who cared what kind of a day I had, every day.

We enjoyed the Chinese food, and munched some bits of a chicken plate with mixed vegetables and rice pilaf, and seeing that I was wiped out from the day, Barbara finally agreed to leave. She was probably more demolished than I was, but being the trooper she was, Barbara kept the vigil all the way. That night, when nine o'clock came, I sent Barbara home.

It was about ten o'clock. I was dozing for the most part. I had the TV on my side of the room playing a movie being shown on HBO. One of the big benefits of moving to Lynfield was that they had basic cable, which meant seventy-some-odd channels, and a premium channel as well. Now I had Pawn Stars, Storage Wars, Ultimate Fighting, and blockbuster movies, some that were pretty new, at my disposal. HBO was featuring Iron Man 2, and although I had seen it, I still enjoyed watching it.

What awakened me was a CNA walking past my bed and calling

ROLAND'S STORY

Willy to wake him up. In the dark, I couldn't see his face, but his English was good, and he spoke with a Spanish accent.

"Mr. Willy! Mr. Willy! Wake up Mr. Willy. It's time to change your diaper." In my semi-wakeful state I wasn't sure that I'd heard the male assistant properly or not. Had he said "change your diaper?"

Willy was waking. "Time to change your diaper, Mr. Willy." I heard the soft rustle of sheets. "Okay, Mr. Willy, I'm going to change your diaper now."

A mild feeling of dread came over me. Dealing with my own bodily functions was admissible. I'd lived with myself, and it's not like that was avoidable. However, this was a different story. Well, it was a large room, with curtains, which the CNA had drawn to completely hide Willy. I was probably not going to notice much at all.

"Okay, Mr. Willy, let's roll you over on your side." The CNA talked Willy through the entire process like he was a toddler, verbalizing every step. "Roll... that's it... okay now come on back... yes, that's it... "

Suddenly the wave hit me. It seemed to literally warm the room, increasing the temperature several degrees. Man, that couldn't be possible... could it? The smell invaded the room completely, leaving no escape. For the smell to be so intense, it was easy to imagine that it was a substance in the air, creeping along like a toxic waste with its poisonous emissions permeating the atmosphere. I felt a bit nauseous, and suppressed an impulse to gag. Oh my God! If we could just open the window.

I waited as ten full minutes ticked away on the clock mounted above the TV. The unnamed CNA had gotten away with his life. The event had left me beaten as if I had been overtaken by the killer fog, and left nearly lifeless. In my mind, the deadly beast had spared me as it had passed, slowly moving out the door, and down the hall, stalking more victims as it sought to make its way. I wanted to take a deep breath, but couldn't imagine that the coast was clear. The entire scene had been more than just a casual ordeal. It was sad that the most memorable event to mark my first day at Lynfield was Willy's diaper change.

My face broke out into a grin. The whole thing was really a plot suitable for a modern day comedy. I started to laugh and, for a moment, thought that a laugh spasm was going to be my wrap up. But as tickled by the whole thing as I was, the spasm, like the killer fog demon, failed to take me. I suppose that Willy's diaper change wasn't that funny after all.

I finally got my deep breath, and sighed, glad it was over. I was ready for a good night's sleep. I was left with the final uneasy thought that, with Willy as my roomie, this wasn't the last time that I would face the killer fog.

14

PTS, OTS, DIETICIANS, & NURSES

I imagined that breakfast hour was eight o'clock.

As I stretched, the TV was still on, playing some kind of paid special TV announcement about an aerobic workout program, geared toward enticing the watcher to buy the whole program at a super discount. If they purchased before the end of the show, they could qualify for the bonus gift, which was worth practically as much as the program. As a special second bonus, just because you were so special for watching the show, they would throw in a free DVD SERIES of their signature protein diet plan, with secrets from the Far East only available on this video that would keep you healthy and strong.

The unseen announcer would enthusiastically encourage viewers, "All this was being offered as a great value with a scary price tag, available exclusively at an outrageous discount, not just this price, (big "X" through the price)…

"And not that price (another "X" through), and no, not even the extremely slashed price here (another "X")...

"But now for a limited time you can enjoy all of this, with bonus one, and bonus two, for the unbelievably low price of... " And the announcer would announce a price that was just on the edge of, "Might as well buy; it's cheap."

Two percent of the channel flippers would see the array of beautiful, healthy, happy bodies, and stay to watch them perform what only Olympic-class athletes could do, with maybe one-half of one percent actually reaching for a credit card.

It was a numbers game, and once the whole thing was created, the equation was simply a few dollars an hour for cheap cable airtime, times a bulk cost of reproducing DVDs, plus shipping, subtracted from the cash flow from the number of units sold, and you could make a few bucks while sitting by your doughboy pool, eating hamburgers, and drinking a beer. After a couple of weeks, you'd pay for the cost of commercial production, and then it was all profit. It was just marketing.

It was only six A.M., but the same voice that had awakened me at ten the night before came in to kick-start Willy and prepare him for breakfast. I got a better look at the carriage they used to mobilize Willy, and was impressed with its simplicity and practicality. I was sure that some medical supplier probably had something that was available for hundreds, or more likely thousands, of dollars that only an insurance company could afford.

But in Willy's carriage they had created something that could have been built from a pencil sketch, forty feet of PVC pipe, some corners and joint fittings, glue, and four six inch hard rubber wheels. I figured that a creative hobbyist or handyman could make it for a hundred bucks. Willy was dressed and loaded into this contraption in about five minutes, and was left waiting for a few minutes before the CNA returned to propel him down the hall to the dining room.

A little after seven-thirty they brought my breakfast on a tray much like the hospital's, and set it on a bed table, also like the hospital. I was familiar with the setup, and so I felt comfortable. With a few changes, it was the same facility kitchen presentation. The fake butter came in a sliced "pat," not a tub. And the juice was in a regular plastic cup, not an "Ocean Spray" prepackaged serving. And, the utensils were metal. Lynfield was scoring points on sight alone. But the best part was that the food was really pretty good, and in decent portions.

Meeting the doctor was fairly uneventful, although he seemed like a genuinely nice guy, and was definitely not a sourpuss. The day nurse was nice, but not a standout personality to mention. But the therapists were a different story altogether.

My PT's name was Irene. She seemed too young to be in her position. I pictured her more as a trainee or a student. As time went on my opinion of her ability was to change a lot. The OT assigned to me was a tall, wonderful, warm lady named Sandra. She and I would get to know each other quite well for a patient-therapist relationship.

Each of my therapists came into my room and performed physical assessments of my condition before designing a plan for my recovery. It was going to be the next day that I really got to work.

During a brief tour they introduced me to several other therapists, showed me stationary cycles, parallel bars, special belted standing machines, and workout benches. One thing that caught my interest was something they referred to as "E-stim." This was a device that was designed to deliver electronic stimulation into muscles and muscle groups by sending a controlled charge of current between two probe points. I imagined that something like that could do a lot for a system based on electrical impulses.

I was to get very familiar with most of this equipment as the weeks progressed. The focus was to put weight on my leg to strengthen the muscles surrounding my knee for standing, and to stretch my right arm and perform weight-bearing exercises to get movement and control to return.

With some experimentation, I was able to determine that when I could get my knee joint completely locked in a straight position I could actually stand with very little additional help. But I also knew that the muscles around my knee had terribly deteriorated to the point that when I tried to stand the knee would fold inward and forward, and the weakened muscles would not cooperate to straighten it. I would have to wake those muscles up and build them up again.

The routine began, and during the course of the week I showed I was a willing participant in rehab. I would opt for extra minutes on the cycle, and keep standing with therapist help until they needed a rest as much as I did.

I felt as though I was making some progress, but it was at a snail's pace. I still had no movement in my right arm, other than the contraction that they referred to as tone. My leg was also building so slowly that the most I could do after a week was just turn my leg inward a bit while lying on my back. The therapists' goal for me was to get me to take a few steps on my own. That was far off in my perspective.

The only way I could do something resembling stepping was to have my left hand on a rail while one therapist sat to my right and behind me, applying two-handed pulling pressure on my knee to compensate for the knee muscles that were MIA. Then, I could

ROLAND'S STORY

put nearly all of my weight briefly on the right leg while I stepped with my left.

The therapist would scoot her stool forward as the other stood by, moving the wheel chair behind me in case I needed to sit, and alternately rush back in front of me to spot my forward progress. The problem, as I anticipated, was that I couldn't bring my right leg forward. As hard as I tried, I wasn't able to shift my weight to my left side enough to allow my right leg to swing clear and perform its half of the two-step process.

So Sandra, sitting on the stool, and in control of my right knee, would let go of her knee-lock, do her best to lift my leg as she kicked my foot forward, and then re-establish the two-handed grip to lock my knee in position. They would cheer for me at the end on this ordeal, and sometimes we would back up and start again.

What started out as an opportunity to find faster and more effective ways to heal me had become a tedious, exhausting process to show me more of what I couldn't do. My logic was simple - if my knee could hold straight, my leg could easily support my weight.

So I needed to find a method of building strength in my knee. I didn't want to appear to stand, especially if it was going to take two hands other than my own to get my leg to cooperate. I wanted to stand on my own. I didn't care if it took longer. But unless they could figure out a way to replace Sandra on her stool, I felt that all of this was mostly just a waste of time.

That's when Stacy came up with an idea. I had been using a gadget called an "AFO," which stands for "ankle-foot orthosis." Someone else had left it with the rehab department after their stint in the care center, and although it didn't fit perfectly, it helped me to stand. It was a stiff synthetic piece that straps on below the knee, and was devised to run down the back of the calf, cup the heel, and run under the entire foot, with a second strap to hold the ankle, foot, and heel in place.

When used, it supported the ankle, and kept the foot from dropping forward. The practical application for me was to keep my foot raised as I took steps, in order to not interfere with walking, and also to be supportive of standing upright.

Stacy was pretty sure that Medi-Cal would cover the cost of orthotics, and a brace as well. At her suggestion, we applied for both. I guess they were fairly commonly requested, because in a day or two, Stacy announced she had scheduled me for an appointment to be fitted for an AFO and a leg brace. I was fortunate to have Stacy around. She was definitely doing what she said she would. She was watching over me.

Every day, the therapists would come to my room, load me into a wheelchair, and roll me to the workout room, housing all those fun machines and devices. As part of the routine, they often came together, sharing time, because often what they were doing with me required two therapists. I felt a bit cheated time-wise, because, although it was a strenuous workout, the overall workout time for me was cut in half.

Other times, they would place me in a standing machine with a harness that basically would capture my butt in a sling and lift me into a standing position with my knees braced from the front. Electrically powered, it was a simple thing to load me into this, and let me stand until I would start to shake. Over the weeks, I would build myself up to twenty minutes of this. But I didn't see it as that helpful. It was like stacking building blocks in a woodworking vise. Either way, there was nowhere to go.

An interesting process involved that device they referred to as the E-stim. Electrodes were attached to me to span specific muscles, and mild electric current would be sent between the two points, making the muscles contract, then relax, repeatedly. This was another low maintenance maneuver, and required very little expertise on the part of a therapist.

I did like the stationary cycle. At least while cycling I could ask for a harder level of peddling resistance, or more time. I could also concentrate on working my right leg more. As with most leg workouts, my disability showed itself in different ways.

On the cycle, my previously bowed legs were now a mismatch, because my right knee now looked like the joint had been installed improperly. It rather looked as though my right leg was sympathizing with my left leg, both curving the same direction. Hence, the new challenge was keeping my lame knee from pounding the center structure of the stationary cycle on every rotation. One day while being set up on the cycle, I met the PT named Kim.

Sandra and I came rolling into the main workout room with the intention of using the cycle. There was one lady on it already, and her time was almost up. The room was hopping with people, with every station being occupied. Sandra wheeled me close to the cycle and placed dibs for me to use it next.

As we waited, Sandra was introducing me to some therapists and the patients in their care. We made our way around the room, and Sandra motioned toward a petite brunette working with an older man named John. They sat near the end of the parallel bars, and I could tell something wasn't right. John looked as if he were about to explode. He apparently was not able to accomplish the task before him.

"... and this is Kim, and this is John," said Sandra.

Kim gave us a quick smile, and a "Hi!" and directed her attention back to John, whose arms were draped across his lap, and he wore a frown, with pursed lips.

"Come on, John, I know you're frustrated, so just stomp your feet!

Go ahead, stomp that one!" John stomped. His anger was obvious. "Stomp the other one!" He stomped. "That one! Stomp 'em! Stomp!"

John was alternately pounding hit feet faster and faster, and louder and louder. People were pausing and turning to see what was going on. John was pounding feverishly now, garnering energy and bursting outward, exhausting himself.

He had captured the entire room's attention, and we all stared, some of us with mouths open. When he finally appeared to be spent, John sagged in his seat, and started to laugh hilariously, and noticing that everyone's eyes were on him, he laughed even more. His feet splayed out in front of him, his engine out of steam, but most importantly, his anger was gone from him.

The room came alive with patients and therapists alike, applauding and cheering like they were at the finish line of a marathon, his transition into joy contagious, bringing on a chorus of laughter. The noise subsided, and people gradually returned to their tasks, the room taking back its nature of a buzzing beehive rather than a rocket launch.

John still sat with legs outstretched. Kim was speaking to him softly, and he maintained a smile that reflected the birth of something deeper and unseen. John had climbed his mountain today, and after that exhibition, I wanted to climb mine, too.

I caught Kim's eye, and silently mouthed the words, "That was awesome!" Kim understood, and in acknowledgment, her eyes squinted, teeth exposed in a powerful smile, shrugged her shoulders, and performed a perfect rapid-fire mini-clap, soundless in the buzzing room, but echoing in the ether.

Sandra helped me arrange my feet in the pedals of the cycle and started me on my workout. I wasn't racing up an impossible hill in my mind, but I was reasonably sure that I was spinning a bit more forcefully than the day before.

ROLAND'S STORY

Barbara continued to visit me daily, arriving late in the afternoon after her work day was over. She kept me in sugar-free treats, clean t-shirts and workout shorts, and on the days that the menu was lacking, provided accents to dinner, or complete substitutions.

In my second week at Lynfield, I was curious to note that pepperoni pizza was the main course for dinner. Although I loved pizza, because of my diabetes, I avoided it most of the time. When I did partake, I balanced the meal with a huge salad and limited my pizza to two slices.

I asked to speak to a nutritionist, because I couldn't believe that pizza was an acceptable dietary choice. Bread was the problem. I was told repeatedly by doctors to limit bread, rice, and pasta. I was okay limiting bread and pasta, as much as I loved them. But rice! My practiced response was, "Doc! See this face? Notice the slanted eyes? Asking me to stop eating rice is like asking a monkey to give up bananas."

I was visited by a young Asian man from the kitchen who turned out to be the head nutritionist for the kitchen. Checking my charts regarding diet, he assured me that the pizza they served met the criteria making it appropriate for me to eat.

So, I figured I might as well try it. At least I was in the right place if I had a problem. I hadn't really noticed any issues with food, but the periodic visits to a clinic doctor determined that my condition required the twice daily addition of Metformin, a common diabetes medicine that helped control sugar levels in blood.

Occasionally, when my blood sugar level was too high, the nurse would give me an injection of insulin, which would take care of it somehow. My days of stopping at the 99 Cent Store to buy three candy bars for less than a buck were over. Too bad. It was such a good deal to add to a two dollar movie.

PTS, OTS, DIETICIANS, & NURSES

My dinner was brought to me just as Barbara was walking through the door of my room. We shared a kiss, and brief updates on the day. I got to hear about the ridiculousness of retail management, and she got to hear about my adventures in rehab. She had brought a small side salad for herself. It was time to inspect the notorious "biscuit pizza," as it was described on the menu.

I began my preview noting the regular meal tray features. As with every meal, there was a small cup of sliced watermelon and cantaloupe that was challenge of its own, often tipping over, spilling melon chunks everywhere. Each meal came with a glass of water, a smaller glass of what I supposed was watered down instant juice substitute, and a small carton of milk. Other than these dining standards, there was the main meal plate, covered by the same kind of flying saucer cover as the hospital had used.

Removing the flying saucer, I was shocked. But I really had no right to be. They called it a "biscuit pizza," and that's exactly what it was. Six inches wide, and nearly an inch thick, with a thin layer if tomato sauce, a sprinkling of some grated mozzarella, and four thin slices of pepperoni.

Yeah, that's the menu had said. What amazed me was what the facility's dietician thought was an appropriate side dish to this huge chunk of biscuit-turned-pizza - a ten inch long, buttered bread stick! No salad, no vegetables... just bread. The sauce, cheese and pepperoni could have added little more than two ounces to the meal, and that was probably an exaggeration.

Barbara and I both thought the presentation was weird. From a mere esthetics point of view, a piece of lettuce or parsley to add some color would have been nice. But there was nothing else on the plate, colorful or not. The sad thing was, it wasn't even that tasty. An extraordinary biscuit pizza, with killer crust, fantastic sauce, gobs

ROLAND'S STORY

of cheese, and heaped with pepperoni would have been worth the wait. But this was just a disappointment.

Now, it wasn't a matter of the nutritionist having a lapse in judgement and designing a bad meal. I now questioned every credential the man had, including the one that most people achieved just to be able to know simple things, like this sign means men's room, and that sign means ladies, and those things that were common sense.

I learned later that Lynfield was part of a huge national chain, and that the monthly menu was dictated by a higher authority than my in-house nutritionist. That just made my overall impression worse. Instead of one man lacking in simple good judgment, there was an elite dietician/nutritionist governing the entire corporate chain of facilities, or maybe a specially screened and selected team of experts, that was dictating menu choices like biscuit pizza with bread sticks for diabetes patients, and dozens or maybe hundreds, of trained specialists all endorsing the serving of this pitiful catastrophe that they referred to as dinner.

I ate all of my pizza, and most of my bread stick, too, offering a piece of it to Barbara to eat with her salad. We both agreed that as far as bread sticks went, it was actually pretty good. That was more than I could say for the pizza. A large bagel was the same size, and much more appetizing. It was a very dry meal, for after all, it was a biscuit, and I had to wash every bite down with milk or water.

Barbara left shortly after dinner, since she was getting backed up on household duties. I didn't mind. I knew that she was sacrificing taking care of herself, and probably losing sleep just so that she could spend some time with me each day. I was getting pretty set in my own routine of visiting with Barbara, or watching a show on my laptop with her, until it was time for her to leave. The routine included checking TV stations on the "house network," and

PTS, OTS, DIETICIANS, & NURSES

if nothing looked like it was worth watching, I'd switch to Netflix on my laptop, where I had my choice of hundreds of movies and documentaries.

That night, I wasn't feeling too well. I had a stiff feeling in my shoulders, and my muscles ached. I decided to call for the nurse. I couldn't concentrate on whatever show I was watching, and my body aches got worse. With the nurse coming, I just tried to relax, hoping that the aches would go away, and maybe I could just sleep.

The nurses were busy performing their nightly rounds of meds distribution, so it took fifteen minutes for her to get to me. Noriko was a nice lady, and knew her stuff. She could tell I was distressed when she saw me.

"How are you feeling, Mr. Takaoka? What seems to be the problem?" She was busy as she talked, feeling my forehead, and quickly checking my face and hands for color. Before I could tell her my symptoms, she had the blood pressure collar on my left arm, and was preparing to check my blood.

"Well, I'm feel achy, and my head feels weird... I'm not exactly dizzy, but I just want to sleep." I explained as best I could.

"Are you nauseated? Do you want throw up?" she queried.

"If I do, will you bring me a new dinner?" I joked, but knowing about the biscuit pizza fiasco, she had no idea that there was more to the joke.

"Oh, are you hungry? We can get you a snack."

"No, no, I'm kidding. I couldn't eat a thing."

"Hmmm. Your blood pressure is a little high, but not too bad." She was cleaning a spot on my finger to prepare for a lancing to get a drop of blood for sampling. The sample taken, she used the same alcohol wipe to clean off any excess blood, and was done in seconds. Her hand-held monitoring device was giving its calculation

ROLAND'S STORY

on my blood sugar level, and she held it close to her face to read the results. "Two hundred-thirty-one..."

"Good grief, I've never been that high! Must've been that biscuit pizza." I exclaimed.

"Yes... okay. Oh, you had the biscuit pizza? I should give you about six units of insulin, and you should be okay. One moment, Mr. Takaoka." And she hustled out of the room to get my injection.

Moments later, she had given me a painless injection that probably hadn't taken a full second to deliver. She also stood by and diligently watched as I swallowed the contents of a small paper cup containing my regular meds. Indicating that I was to summon her if my condition did not improve in an hour, she hurried off to the rest of her stops.

I was as miserable as I had been since the day of my stroke. That was something to be said about strokes. Other than the torture of stretching and therapy moves, I was experiencing very little pain of any kind. It wasn't as though I'd broken my arm or leg, or ripped muscles. The arm and leg had just ceased functioning, leaving half of me a limp Raggedy Andy.

It was exhausting putting up with the soreness of shoulder and neck muscles. I really wasn't clear whether the biscuit pizza had been responsible. But I knew I had no need to test it twice. Next time I'd get the cheeseburger.

15

FARTHER DOWN THE RABBIT HOLE

By the next morning, the neck and shoulder aches had passed. I felt pretty normal, considering that my definition of normal had changed radically and abruptly a little more than five weeks ago.

I concentrated on getting stronger and more flexible. Along with muscles that just didn't seem to be working, I had muscles that worked when I didn't want them to.

A tickle or an itch scratched just right could elicit movement in my arm or leg or both that I couldn't duplicate on command. On top of that, there was atrophy in muscles from non-use. I was constantly battling a leg that tended to pull up behind me when I tried to stand, and an arm that pulled involuntarily across my chest, and a hand that was usually closed in a contorted version of a conventional fist, that had to be coaxed carefully into an open position.

The event of the night before made it clear that I would have to determine what foods I could eat, and what foods I should avoid, even if a diet professional indicated it was okay for me to partake. Obviously, that was something I couldn't rely on. But under the circumstances, perhaps I could use this hazardous arrangement to my advantage.

Since I was in a perfect environment to be monitored, and summon help if I needed it, I decided to take advantage of a nutrition team that would offer me waffles, pancakes, French toast, bacon, cheeseburgers, french fries, ham, country fried potatoes, au gratin potatoes, mashed potatoes and gravy, spaghetti with meat sauce, lasagna, rice, and bread sticks, and stand by with medical support if required.

I was determined to try anything that sounded good, and test my physical reactions while it was safe to do so. I'd prepare to add anything to the official ban list, alongside the biscuit pizza, should it prove to be a problem.

The daily grind in therapy proved to be helpful. But something kept telling me that we were missing the boat. The therapists were good, pleasant to work with, and I could tell they were devoted to their jobs. However, what I wanted was a plan that helped me get stronger. Right now, I felt like Pinocchio with half my strings cut. The puppet masters were trying to rack me and stack me so I looked like I was standing and walking, but I couldn't really do it on my own.

I didn't want the impression that I was walking, but rather a method of learning to crawl, and work up from there. I couldn't lift my leg, let alone take a step. It just didn't make sense. The equation was wrong, and the figures didn't add up. I still attacked the work the therapists gave me with dedication. Although I saw no substantial progress, I had to believe the effort was making a difference.

I found myself on another typical rehab morning on a machine in the workout room, The E-stim lady was zapping my leg muscles as I powered a stationary bike. Sandra was busying herself with arranging various implements and assorted machine attachments. It seemed they were never returned to their proper places by staff members. Voices in the distance were alternately between harshness and encouragement.

I could barely make out, "Don't touch me! I have cancer all over my body." The voice was getting louder. "I have come here to die, leave me ALONE!"

In spite of these commands, she was being wheeled into the room. A frail looking Kim, the PT who had assisted the "foot stomper" a day before, was speaking to the lady in the chair.

"The doctor has ordered therapy for you. You can still move your arms and legs. Don't you want to walk a little, try to get up, so you can go to the bathroom by yourself? You'll start feeling better."

A difficult case. "What's the use? I am going to die."

They moved to a corner of the workout room, and Kim continued to talk to her. I thought about how impossible a situation it would be to have someone ask you to do something for yourself when you had such a limited amount of time to live. How was Kim going to get a woman's mind to open whose body was closing down? I wondered if the lady had actually been told she was going to die by her doctor.

"Just do this..." I heard Kim say. "Just try this."

It sounded like the grouch was about to give in, and Kim was making some headway. From where I was positioned, facing the other way, I couldn't see what she was having the lady do.

"Okay, that's good. See? Wasn't so tough. Before you know it you'll be driving yourself around everywhere. Tell you what, let's use the rest of our time to show you what the facility looks like.

ROLAND'S STORY

There is a lovely garden with a fountain, and the weather is just perfect right now..."

The skeptical lady, obviously angry at life, was putting on quite a performance, rolling her eyes at Kim's suggestion. I guess she was getting tired of resisting, and grudgingly let Kim roll her out the door towards the garden.

I looked at Sandra, who was checking my progress, and said, "Man, Kim has a hard job, there. You get many people like that? Is she actually terminally ill?"

"Well, we're not allowed to discuss the details of other patient's conditions. You're welcome to ask her if you want." She raised her eyebrows, and they said everything.

Fat chance I was going to have any kind of conversation with the grouch, let alone a pleasant one. Sandra was being honest. Although staff members were not allowed to discuss other patients with anyone in therapy, the patients were free to do as they pleased and could talk to anyone. My sessions for the day were over, and Sandra was wheeling me back to my room. It was right at the five o'clock dinner hour when I was rolling up to my room. Suddenly there was a commotion approaching from down the hall, coming right at us.

"Put me back in there! Put me back in there! I don't wanna go!" The voice got louder as the distance closed.

The man pushing the wheelchair was a CNA, and was remaining extremely calm. "Don't you want to see your friends and have dinner? They're waiting for you."

The husky little ball of fire was bristling for a fight, but she was apparently in a condition that prevented her from rising out of the wheelchair and picking one with her captor. He kept moving

FARTHER DOWN THE RABBIT HOLE

her along, and the volume of the interaction grew distant as they continued down to the dining room.

The fire ball was aflame. "Put me back in there! Put me back in there!"

I was beginning to realize that there was much more to this facility than just a rehab. As Sandra wheeled me into my room, I heard another familiar voice ringing out. "... To the shores of Tripoli..."

Oh, Lord.

"... Air and on the sea. If the Army and the Navy, hmm hmm, dada..."

Where did he get those words!

"...The United States Marines."

All I could think was, what a menagerie. I'd better fix my body soon, or I stood the chance of losing my mind while I gained my body back. Somehow getting my arm and leg back in exchange for my sanity didn't strike me as a fair deal.

To keep myself from reacting with irritation, I had to reason with myself. For one thing, I hadn't yet resorted to feeling sorry for myself, and that was a good sign. Not that I liked being away from home this way. I felt like Alice, stepping through the looking glass, and all the characters were donning different masks, hats, and personalities.

But the parallel of finding myself wandering in "Wonderland" was almost too real. This was my version of a one-way trip down the rabbit hole, and the only way back was forward. I started realizing that sometimes the shortest route was the long way around.

I guess this formula for thinking wasn't exactly the application of reason. However, it kept me from comparing my present status to what my life had been like before the stroke, and wondering

ROLAND'S STORY

where I would have been had this not happened. Many days back at Saint Michael's I had wondered what I did wrong.

It wasn't like I was a self-destructive person, or didn't care about health and fitness. But whenever my thoughts traveled that course, they had nowhere to go. After a while, I realized that it was pointless to pursue that line of thinking. There was nothing reasonable that availed itself to me so that I could put the issue to rest. I didn't know why I was here. All I knew for certain was that I was here.

Or, maybe I'd wake up one day from a long dream and find that my highly developed imagination had allowed me to think up this whole "Wonderland" adventure.

Okay, probably not. I was trapped in reality, not a dream, and the only road seemed to be a hard one. I knew I would not give up hope. But I was getting a little desperate for a sign.

The inspiration event of the week was when Kim, the PT, had raised a ruckus and enticed a foot stomping session out of John. Why couldn't we see that sort of thing every day?

I thought about the lady that was presumably dying of cancer. That had to be the hardest. It seemed Kim might have been making some headway, even with the grouch.

So, if someone who had only a short time to live could even grudgingly agree to try just a little, I had no excuse. I made up my mind to fully commit to rehabilitation, and maybe keep my eyes, heart, and mind open for some inspiration along the way.

You never know... maybe from the higher ground, we might even have a sighting of a miracle or two.

16

A NEW CHALLENGE

A few days had passed. Routine. Barbara's visits, and more routine.

We had some fun moments watching a short show each day, and she was always bringing something to accent my dinner and make it more interesting. Routine kept us timely, and Barbara got to go home early enough to finish household things, and get to bed at a reasonable time. My workouts were getting more intense, simply because I was building up basic body strength. It was progress, but I had to keep my expectations in check. Expecting just a little improvement made the noticeable progress acceptable, and kept my frustrations at bay.

Healthcare facility food was becoming an interesting hobby. I was happy to discover that French toast and waffles went down fine. Surprisingly, spaghetti with meat sauce had no ill-effect, and was actually quite good. The portions were more substantial at Lynfield than they were at Saint Michael's. So, many times, Barbara

ROLAND'S STORY

brought a Mexican grilled chicken salad, or something similar, and we'd split both the meal she brought and the menu selection, making the variety quite interesting.

The dining techniques I had developed at Saint Michael's were improved upon by the upgrade of metal utensils. Now the springiness that was prevalent with plastic ware was replaced by steel steadfastness. This reduced my prep time, cutting food down to size, and maybe even made the food taste a bit better. However, it may have just been my attitude.

Along with the spaghetti dinner, there were a few meals to look forward to. The soft shell taco wasn't bad. Stuffed bell peppers were the best. It seemed that the chefs had taken lessons in baked salmon from the crew at Saint Michael's, and after two tries, I steered clear of fish dishes altogether. So a few items on the menu were added to the banned list, and everything else was either acceptable or a treat. In this way, food became a non-issue.

The landmark development at Lynfield was that, in getting stronger, my balance improved. Inside of two weeks, I was mastering the job of cleaning after my trips to the john. After that, anxieties about having to go home and ask Barbara for help with this issue were considerably diminished. This had quite an impact on my overall mindset, and my confidence increased. Arm and leg progress still inched along, but I started believing that it had to amount to something.

One morning, no therapists came before lunch. Usually one or the other or both came to get me by eleven o'clock, to leave me sweaty by lunch time. I decided to enjoy my lunch, and if they came too early, they would have to wait.

At about twelve-thirty, as I sat close to the entrance to my room in my wheelchair eating lunch, my back to the door, I could hear

A NEW CHALLENGE

a conversation clearly between a new patient and someone else. His room was directly across from mine.

Normally, all I could hear was mumbles and overtones. Today, because I chose to sit in the wheelchair, I was on the far side of my table. So I had to leave my curtain open and carefully position myself, to not be in the way of traffic in and out of the room. Being so close, I could make out every word.

They had brought him in just two days before, a big guy with a deep voice. He must have been in some serious pain from the sounds he made, and I hadn't heard him be cheerful or laugh. He would often shout out like they were truly torturing him. The conversation I listened to at that moment was congenial, and he definitely didn't sound like the huge bear that I'd been listening to complain of pain. I found myself eavesdropping.

"No, you don't have to get up. Let's roll you on your side." I recognized Kim, and thought it was just her luck to get stuck with that big wounded bear.

"It usually takes two people to do that." He said.

"We have two people; you and me!" I heard her say. I could hear them both snickering. I was joining in the fun, and they were not even aware. I had a momentary spasm, and had to pause from trying to chew my pork chop, being careful so that when I did get to inhale it wouldn't include a chunk of meat.

I could hear a light punching sound. "Pound harder," said the bear in low tones. This continued for several minutes. I was finishing my lunch. Then their conversation resumed.

"My dad used to do that to me," he said. "When I was a kid. Now he's passed away." Their conversation continued, but hall noise increased, and drowned them out. I felt a little sheepish for having listened in. But I had a thought which I somehow knew was

ROLAND'S STORY

significant. Whatever magic Kim possessed, she had used it to tame and sooth the wounded bear.

I was feeling drowsy from my meal, and my head was drooping forward. I wasn't prone to sleeping in a sitting position, but that's probably because I could always just lie down anytime I wanted to. Now, I could do it, but it was a lot more work.

Just then Kim walked in, surprising me out of my daze. "Hi, Roland!" She said in greeting, giving me a warm smile. "Enjoy your lunch?"

I took a deep breath to feed my brain some oxygen. "Hi, Kim. What are you, working through your lunch?"

"No, I ate earlier," she said.

I tried to stretch as inconspicuously as I could in order to get my blood flowing. "But I heard you in there with the guy across the hall."

"Oh, yeah. Ted hasn't been eating because he has so much pain. So I took a short lunch, and thought I'd go help him deal with it." Ted. His name was Ted. He was a bear after all. A Teddy Bear! My wonderland menagerie was growing with new characters.

"I see... that's cool. So, you are assigned to him as his therapist, then." I said this as much a question as a statement.

"Yes, but not originally." She seemed a little hesitant to talk about it further, and I did not press, for obviously we were discussing another patient, and that, as I remembered, was not allowed. "But anyway, I was asked to sit in for Irene, who is absent today. They asked me to work with you. Is that okay?"

I was startled. "Uh, yeah! That's fine. Actually, I'd love to do this. Let's go!" I felt a tingle of excitement just to have a change of pace. An interaction with a new therapist was uncharted territory.

"Okay, then!" Kim arranged the leg attachments to my wheelchair,

A NEW CHALLENGE

helped me hoist my right foot onto the footrest, and we started out the door and down the hall, making our way to the workout room.

"So, tell me, Roland. You've been doing a lot of cycling, and I see you in the standing frame sometimes. They have you doing some walking. Right?" Kim was getting to know about the routines the therapists had already established with me.

"Well, if you want to call that walking, I guess I can fly, too." I was a little sour on the walking idea, because I didn't think that a balancing act like the one we performed, with two therapists in hands-on assist mode was truly valid.

"So, why do you say that?" Kim asked.

It seemed I'd expressed this a dozen times. "Kim, I've told the therapists that if my knee could hold itself straight I'd be walking now, or at least standing with no help needed. I've asked them to teach me what to do to strengthen my knee muscles, and no one seems to want to give me that. I think the cycling kinda helps, but there has to be a better way. And I really want to wake up my right arm. All I've been able to do is shrug my shoulder a bit."

I was bordering on frustration. I didn't want to be negative, but when she asked, it felt like I'd been holding back for months. Well, I guess it was almost two months since my stroke, so that really wasn't a false assumption. I felt like someone was finally listening to me. I had kept a positive attitude, but I wasn't getting the results I had hoped for.

"Okay, and what are some of the things you notice as your biggest challenges when doing standing and stepping exercises?" she asked.

That was easy. When the therapists had me stand for any length of time, my lower back began to hurt. Plus, just getting into a straight standing position was torturous, trying to straighten from

ROLAND'S STORY

my inclined bed position, or the wheelchair slouch seemed unnatural to me after all these weeks.

"I can tell exactly what bugs me most. My back. It's hard to get straight, and when I do, afterward it's my back that pays. I spend all my time in bed, or in this chair. Either way, I'm bent for long periods of time, and it's hard to straighten out, especially under the pressure of trying to stand up straight for everyone, and my back compounds the problem. Uh... sorry, I didn't mean to go off." It was the first time I had allowed myself the luxury of anything resembling a complaint.

"It's okay. Sometimes we just have to tell it like it is." Kim wasn't offended. I guess she had plenty of more severe attitudes to deal with. "I tell you what, let's try something different today. Have they gotten you on your hands and knees? Done anything like that?"

"Never." I said. I wasn't even sure if I could get into that position with a bum leg and arm on the same side of my body.

"Alright, we're going to try it." Kim wasn't acting overly enthusiastic like a cheerleader, but was very "matter of fact," about the idea.

We got to the workout room, and there were a couple of therapists with their patients doing the usual workouts. We picked a corner, and Kim parked the wheelchair. Then she selected a gait belt and strapped it around my body a few inches above my waist.

"Do you think you can move from your chair to the floor if we put a mat down over there?" She pointed to an open area of the room.

"I don't know, but let's try it." I was in the mood to push myself, and trying something new was appealing.

"Okay, now I want you to slide to your right knee, pivoting and end up with the top of your body leaning in the chair. Do you think you can do that? There are a couple of people here to help out if we need them."

A NEW CHALLENGE

"Uh... yeah, I think so." I felt the slack taken up on the gait belt, and Kim was guiding my body in its pivot action. After a few seconds, I was on both knees and facing the back of my wheelchair, elbows in the seat, leaning comfortably and feeling stable.

It felt wonderful. "You okay?" asked Kim.

"I feel great!" I said. "First time I've been in this position in two months."

"Alright, so let's give it a couple minutes, and let your body adjust," said Kim. "Breathe, Roland, take some nice easy breaths."

I took a few deep breaths, and could feel muscles all over my body relax. It surprised me how good I felt. "You can start a new profession. Call it Wheelchair Yoga," I joked. We both had a chuckle at the thought.

"Actually, I teach yoga. I meet with a group in the park, and we do stretching, some yoga, and exercise. I was thinking maybe of getting a website, but I don't know anything about that stuff."

"Hey! That's my profession. I'm a web designer. Come by my room sometime, and I'll give you a little tour." I was feeling good from the workout session. But an opportunity to help Kim, especially when she was impacting my workout like she was, tickled me, and I wanted to give her a better idea of what she could do with her own site.

"You're kidding! You design websites?" I was nodding in an animated fashion, so she could see the answer was 'yes' from behind me. "That's awesome! I'm going to have to take you up on that. I don't know the first thing, except that I think I need one."

"Well, that IS the first thing. Knowing that you need one. We'll talk more about it." The idea of helping her made me feel good. I planted it in my mind that I'd come up with a way to help her without having to charge much.

"Okay, Roland. Now, get ready to put your arms down straight

ROLAND'S STORY

and go to a hands and knees position." I did as she directed, and found myself in Wheelchair Yoga, Position 2.

Kim assisted my resistant right arm to a spot on the floor, and I was on all fours. Then she was directing me further, and before long I was on my stomach, my back arched backwards, elbows on the floor. It felt amazing. "Now you've got weight-bearing on your shoulder, and a good stretch for your back going on at the same time. Are you okay like that?"

"Yup. Good to go. I needed this." I felt as though I was finally being challenged. It seemed that Kim had that effect on people. It thrilled me to be doing something new, and not part of the established routine.

When I had been in that position for five minutes or more, Kim indicated it was time to get back in the chair. She talked and assisted me back to my hands and knees. From there, I found myself almost standing, Kim nearly carrying me as I tried to maneuver my body to land back in my wheelchair. In a few seconds I was again seated, a little askew, breathing like I'd been pressing weights. Kim was a little flushed, but smiling at our accomplishment. What I had assumed was a frail little lady was actually a wiry, strong woman.

It was the most exhilarating feeling that I had had since my stroke, and without trying to measure the achievement, I knew that we'd raised the bar on my therapy. With Kim's help and insightful creativeness, I had found some relief for my stiff, sore back, and performed some tasks that I had not been asked to do before. It was like successfully completing my first back flip on the trampoline.

I guess the best way for me to describe it was that I wanted to conquer my mountain the way the "foot stomper" had a few days earlier, and Kim had pointed me to the mountain and turned me loose. Maybe it was just a small hill. But it was my hill, and I had climbed it.

17

NIGHT OF THE BANSHEE

As my eighth week was underway, I was a veteran of Lynfield Rehab. I had gotten acclimated to craziness, oddities and, aberrations. People were often depressed or sad. Many people were angry and resentful of life itself for handing them a raw deal. Some were quietly pouting their last days away; some were violently verbal, even combative at times.

There were the rare few people who were enjoying life in spite of their condition. I decided that whatever I did, I would try to emulate the best of them, using the happiest people as my examples, and setting one as well, so that when people spoke of me, the conversation would reflect a good attitude.

And people did speak. It wasn't so much the patients, although there was always that; people were naturally curious why others were in rehab. Long term nursing care was the most common need. People who were at Lynfield for that reason could no longer care for themselves, and had no family or friends who could help. Hence,

ROLAND'S STORY

there was an abundance of people, personalities, and stories being talked about.

The therapists seemed to have a real handle on discretion regarding discussing patients. But there were still nurses, CNAs, and assorted other personnel who would toss idle chatter, sometimes choosing subjects about people who were easily within earshot, and listening as the thoughtless employees expressed opinions or shared something private that, in the name of human decency, should have been withheld.

Such was the nature of the hall clusters of employees who had nothing pressing to attend to, not enough integrity to focus on their work, and lacked the common decency to be civil and compassionate to patients. The basic banter was fairly harmless. But when someone knew they were being talked about, and the comments were derogatory, what was said could have a devastating impact. Critical comments could cause an already negative person to drop lower in their own personal incentive to heal, or even to live.

It was mildly annoying that employees could chatter about something, and it would sound like they were right in your room. Early in the morning, late in the evening, and even in the middle of the night, staff members would talk to patients and coworkers alike as if full volume was universally accepted.

I got used to being awakened at various times of the day, even when sleeping was the more common activity, to hear Willy's name being called out repeatedly so that his failing ears and demented mind could understand. However, it was downright irritating to be watching a show in my room and miss critical movie dialogue, because nurses talking shop and laughing outside my door were so loud that they drowned out the TV.

I supposed that soundproofing the walls in a hospital-type setting could be a serious hazard. If someone called for help, they had to be heard. But that didn't excuse people from speaking inhumanely or cruelly. I learned to live with the sound and chatter. But I never got used to people who could talk out loud with a blatant disregard for human feelings. It was one thing to be loud, and quite another to be inconsiderate, rude, and even mean.

One afternoon I was feeling drowsy once again after hard consecutive workouts with my therapists. I had just eaten lunch, and was sitting with my back to the door again, and could hear several bits of conversation going on up and down the hall. I could hear Ted's voice as he greeted Kim. I guess Ted was bed bound, because his therapy always kept him in his room. I recalled the previous day when two nursing assistants were discussing him as they stood just outside his door.

"Yeah, what a grouch. That guy's a psych patient!" one of the CNAs said.

The other responded, "No kidding. I was just supposed to turn him on his side yesterday. I thought that Neanderthal was going to bite my head off!"

Ted was telling the story to Kim. "Yeah, that's what they said. They act like I'm stupid. I've got a PhD in literature. It's dehumanizing. They judge who I am from the feedback they derive from this environment. I don't exactly feel in the mood for a Library of Congress cocktail party."

"So, what things do you like to read?"

Redirecting the conversation, she was busying herself with some therapeutic activity while he got into his subject. He was obviously a very intelligent man; articulate, and well spoken. They talked during the entire hour of therapy. From the discussion, one would have thought that they were sharing a cup of coffee. But I knew better. From occasional directions she would give him, or short statements regarding progress or soreness or whatever, I could tell Kim was busy the whole time. Ted always ended their sessions with, "Thank you, Kim. God bless you."

So, she tames savage beasts and gets people to climb mountains. I liked my therapists, and they were good. But I'd reached a plateau with them early on, and they had nothing more to incentivize and challenge me. I'd heard that I could request a specific therapist to work with. Although I didn't want to raise any issues with the therapist I'd been working with, I felt Kim had more to offer. I decided to pursue the switch, and not let possible hurt feelings or potential misunderstandings keep me from asking.

That evening I shared my feelings with Barbara, and explained about the possibilities of changing PT's. She agreed that I should take advantage of anything that could advance my healing process. I made up my mind to talk to Stacy about it the next day.

After Barbara left for the night, I settled into my movie watching routine. A couple doors down the hall, a patient had a tendency of calling out to people who walked past her door.

"Hello? Hello! Can you help me? Help me. Please, help me!" A few seconds would pass. "Hello? Can you please help me? Hello!"

There was an odd rhythm to her repeated words. Usually no one stopped. Sometimes, her cries would get more desperate. "PLEASE! HELP ME, SOMEONE!" And someone would stop to see what she needed.

Once she had their attention, her voice calmed, and it became evident that all she wanted was for someone to ask her what she wanted. A few minutes later, after she had quieted, they would leave. And a few minutes after that, she would start in again. "Hello? Hello!"

That night she had been incessantly repeating her message, and after a half dozen people responded, the caller had run out of responders. I lay watching my program, wishing it had a pause control so I could keep from missing the good parts, and maybe replay segments. Being on TV, all I had was a volume control, which I couldn't increase any louder without possibly waking Willy.

No one had responded to the eternal greeter for nearly an hour. I couldn't help myself, and had to admit that I was becoming severely agitated. Why didn't somebody DO something? Maybe she needed a sedative. Couldn't a team of young, professional, well-educated and creative medical staff find a way to bring this unreasonable banter from the banshee to an end? Finally I had had enough.

"Oh, why don't you just shut UP!" I shouted, much louder than I'd intended. I immediately wondered if my exclamation would bring medical personnel into my room to see what my problem was.

"Why don't YOU shut up!" came the reply from the banshee.

Oh, My God! She was actually listening for any response from anywhere, and she was prepared to do battle with any reciprocal party. I could just imagine the Teddy Bear joining in, and Willy busting out a chorus of the Marine's Hymn. It was a scary thought that I might have crossed the line of demarcation, and had perhaps introduced a new concept of outreach to the banshee, who had previously been unaware of my presence. I decided that it would be prudent to drop out of the fight before it got out of hand.

"Shut up! You, shut up! SHUT - UP!" The caller had escalated her message to be an attack on anything that moved, whether it spoke to her or not. My outburst had unintentionally challenged her, and given her new terminology and ammunition to snipe all passersby.

Too late to be neutral, I had to accept my responsibility in the overall scene. Although it was unfortunate and unreasonable to

ROLAND'S STORY

make the entire hall of patients deal with her noise, now accented with a bad attitude that I had helped her achieve, I had to concede defeat, and let go of my cause. I had to question what was more insane - to be seriously annoyed by a crazy person's antics, or engaging with them in an argument.

I switched off the TV, found a Netflix show on my laptop, and put my headphones on. Wisdom can be such a simple thing.

18

VISIONS AND DREAMS

The next day I was picked up by Irene, my PT, and escorted to the workout room. I didn't tell her about my idea of switching therapists. I had sent a message to Stacy asking to speak with her, and thought it best to wait and see what she recommended.

When we arrived in the workout room, there was an assembly of OTs and PTs gathered in a semi-circle, watching as Kim talked to the group.

"They should be through in a few minutes. Do you mind hanging out?" asked Irene.

"No, not at all," I replied, trying to catch up on the subject that Kim was presenting.

"And so we're experimenting with Dance Therapy, because the rhythm facilitates movement by the synchronizing of brainwaves and other bodily activities." As Kim explained, her listeners nodded their heads, some of them because her statement apparently made some kind of sense, and some because it was more desirable than standing there looking clueless.

"This is Anna, and we're just going to play a little rhythmic music for her...." She turned and reached behind her to start a portable CD player. "Anna has had a head injury, and has some issues with balance and limb control, and hasn't been able to stand. She agreed to join us to listen to some cool, popular music that I thought she might like."

The music started. Heavy bass drove the song that I recognized was popular at the time, and most of the therapists, getting into the spirit of things, played along, bobbing to the music, and some of them clapping to the beat.

Suddenly, Anna was going wild in response to the music, began screaming like she was a fan in the front row at a concert. To everyone's surprise, she stood up, laughing hilariously as she danced wildly to the music with almost perfect balance. Shocked, everyone froze for nearly five seconds before they recovered and more enthusiastically resumed clapping hands and dancing along.

Party in the workout room!

It was an amazing sight. After a couple minutes of this, I guess Kim thought she'd better take it easy, and give Anna a rest. She reached for the volume control and gradually brought the song to a premature end, and Anna, her body still gyrating and bouncing, fell into her chair like a rag doll, and several therapists joined in the effort of helping rearrange her into a better sitting position.

Everyone was applauding and cheering. The presentation had lost all sense of order, with some therapists congratulating Anna on her wonderful demonstration, several all talking at once with Kim, who was at somewhat of a loss as to how to address the multiple questions and statements that were inundating her. She just stood there, slack jawed, and looked around in awe.

VISIONS AND DREAMS

Someone noticed the time, and several more patient-therapist combos had joined the line waiting. The party dissolved, but reluctantly, everyone talking in small clusters and some trying to get in a last few words with Kim and Anna.

It was the second time I had witnessed such a commotion with applause and cheering. For a second time, like the first, it had been Kim who was responsible.

Kim hurried out carrying her CD player, saying, "It's time to pick up Jean!" And she was gone.

Irene had hooked me up to the E-stim machine, and my leg tingled with a fluctuating electric current while I stood strapped in a frame. With each turn of electric current, I did my best to engage my muscles, and relaxed into the sling support in between. I was half-way through my session when Kim returned with Jean.

Jean was a big lady. From the looks of her condition, Jean probably suffered from a stroke somewhat like mine. But hers had affected her left side, and mine, the right side. Seeing her with Kim was a bit absurd. Jean obviously outweighed Kim by a significant amount, being both taller and more robust in stature. Kim was petite and probably barely tipped the scale at one-hundred pounds.

I turned to Irene and asked, "How can little Kim manage a woman that size?" It seemed to be a math and physics puzzle, and my brain couldn't negotiate an answer.

"Yeah... there's no way by herself," said Irene. "We have this thing called a Hoyer lift. Have you seen one?"

"I think I know what you're talking about. I see them rolling them down the hall sometimes." I had seen what appeared to be a kind of crane, with a sling attachment.

Irene nodded her head. "Yes. We have a couple of them. They move them from room to room when needed."

ROLAND'S STORY

Jean was a talker. "... And if someone would just bring me my car, I know I could drive and get around." Kim said nothing as she propelled the wheelchair into the workout room, but her eyes were like saucers. "And if I could improve my standing balance just a bit more, I know I could start working as a masseuse again." Kim just smiled.

"What's WRONG with men, Ki-i-i-im..." She added musical flavor singing her name as she said it. "How come we are both single?" I was smiling now. This was one bold lady.

"My daughter has been looking for a date for me on 'Match.com.' She found me a guy who was interested in meeting, and he came by last weekend. I wasn't really interested in him. I don't know... there was something wrong with him."

At that point I lost it, and immediately went into a spasm. No "Hahaha," just the gut wrenching seizure that it seemed I alone in all of humanity was plagued with. Irene had heard me describe my problem, but was unfamiliar with the effect. She stared at me hesitantly, a half-smile teasing her face.

"Is he okay?" I heard Jean ask. I looked up to see both Jean and Kim staring at me, and that simply added to my seizure time.

I waved at them, indicating something that they couldn't translate, and Irene said, "Yeah, I think he's okay." She caught my eye, repositioned her face to be directly in front of me, and raised her eyebrows, as if to say, "Are you?"

I managed to nod a weak affirmative, and waited for the cramp to ease up. The thought of this woman of such formidable physical nature, in a wheelchair as the result of a stroke, having a date in a rehab with guy through Match.com, was almost more than I could take. But the announcement that there was something wrong with HIM -- well, that put me over the top.

VISIONS AND DREAMS

Jean seemed like a wonderful, colorful person. But the absurdity of all that came out of her mouth was the most comical series of lines I had heard since rehab in Lynfield began. By this time, Irene was chuckling too, and so was Kim and Jean. But I doubted that we were all in on the same joke.

We spent the rest of the session smiling, keeping one ear open for bits of words and wisdom that came from the direction of Jean and Kim, a conversation that was mostly one-sided, with a never ending flow of enthusiasm from Jean. Then I was returned to my room, having been mildly challenged and moderately fatigued. But, overall, I was in good humor.

Later that day, Stacy came by my room, and I expressed my wish to work with Kim. She told me this could be arranged. I tried to make it clear that I had no real issues with Irene, but I wished to explore some ideas that I had heard Kim talk about. In order to clear the awkward situation, and preserve the good will I had established with Irene, I sent a message to the therapy department requesting that she stop by when she got the chance. When Irene came by, she was already informed of the switch, and seemed unmoved by the change. So our exchange was brief, and since she seemed fine with my trade, I let the matter go, and allowed myself to get excited about the possibilities of working with Kim.

The next day Sandra came in about mid-morning as usual, and hustled me off to the workout room. "I heard that you're going to be working with Kim today." Her voice was very matter of fact.

"Yeah... do you think Irene is upset with me? It has nothing to do with me being unhappy with her, or anything." I was hoping that she'd be straight with me in case there was any concern.

"No! Oh, no. We have people change therapists a lot, and some people regularly work with more than one PT or OT. It's a matter of being comfortable together, and a lot of other factors." Her words made me feel more at ease. I liked Sandra, and we had done a lot of talking, sharing thoughts on life, at times disregarding the whole subject of rehab.

"Okay, thanks for that." I said. "My intentions do not include accidentally hurting someone's feelings, or being insulting."

"By the way, you know I'm getting married next month, right?"

"Yes, I remember you saying! Congratulations!"

"Well, I just wanted to let you know, in case you're still here, that someone will be standing in for me for a couple weeks. But you may not even be here by then." She said that last line with an air of enthusiasm, suggestive that my condition could be significantly improved.

"True." I said, thinking about a subject that repeatedly crossed my mind. How much longer would I be in rehab? It had to end at some point. Besides, I was trimming the edges of my sanity as it was.

I had undergone an abrupt change of life from an active, competitive, creative person, to an isolated, bed-and-wheelchair captured invalid, struggling to regain some of what I'd lost, just so I could limp into the world that used to be my life.

As we engaged in cycling with the E-stim, part of my regular regimen of activity, I became introspective as I often did. The nature of my existence in rehab facilitated a lot of thought activity. Due to the mixed nature of constituents in rehab and medical environments, I tended to be more reclusive, staying away from the dining room, and not participating in group events or parties.

On that day, my mind wandered back to things my father and mother had said long ago. Dad and I had taken a hard road, him teaching me how to fear God by being His local agent. It was going to take me thirty-five years of my life to resolve my feelings for my dad. After that, Dad and I were the best of friends. The resolution

VISIONS AND DREAMS

came with a simple flipping of a switch in my mind. I discovered the concept of forgiveness.

Once I realized that my dad didn't hate me, and that he only treated me as harshly as he did because his own life had taught him his lessons at a greater cost to him than he wanted me to pay, then suddenly it was easy to forgive. The more I thought about it, the more I realized that my own hatred had been my response to the illusion that my dad was mean for no good reason, or an unjustifiable one.

So, I could clearly see the equation in my head - Awareness brings Understanding, and Understanding clarifies Intention. And, it seemed that when I finally understood my father's intentions, it made everything okay. So, I often reviewed back things my dad had expressed decades ago, and without the illusion of negative intention, I could reevaluate his words. It made me consider the words passed to me by the preacher at a church I had attended, and was a quote from Jesus: "You will know the truth, and the truth will set you free."

The words that my dad spoke when I was about fifteen years of age that resonated with me now were, "We create our own reality, you know." At the time, no, I didn't know. It was to take me the first five decades of my life to even start walking the path of a serious seeker. Having read numerous books, and talked with many people about spiritual and religious concepts, I had developed my own version of what religion was, and my conclusion was that the religion didn't matter so much as the spiritual nature of the individual.

Now, when reviewing dad's words again, it was with a new light. "We create our own reality..."

Maybe we did. But if so, how in the hell did I create this mess that I was in? Surely it couldn't have been a conscious choice to have a stroke, and go through months of medical facility incarceration, while dealing with craziness, and mediocrity as the standard for healing.

ROLAND'S STORY

In my few years of college, I had started out as a math major. It turned out that I hated it. But what I did take away from school was a logical mind. Applying logic to spiritual concepts involved some abstract thinking. This logic presented me with the case that, if I created my own reality, then I created my stroke - if not on purpose, then through some unintentionally used flaw or loophole. Or, maybe I had some misconception of the principles of my logic formula.

As I cycled and E-stimmed, I ran it over in my mind... "We create our own reality." I'd have to give this more time to simmer in the pot.

My mom was an entirely different experience for me than my dad. She and I had a great relationship all my life, from my perspective, anyway. She put up with a kid that sneeked out the back door to go play at someone else's house, and a toddler that saw no reason not to share the big dog's bone, resulting in neighborhood searches and occasional trips to the hospital emergency for stitches. All in all, I was a pretty good kid, and because I feared my dad, I was more of a "mama's boy."

Mom had said four words to me, over and over, that now echoed in my brain, and I felt that they had to be significant in my search for my logical solution. "Spiritual precedes the physical." The way she interpreted this was that what happened to us physically, first happened to us spiritually. So, although I could hang with the order of things in the concept, I just couldn't see how this was particularly useful, when what happened, happened regardless of where it first occurred.

Anyway, I was sort of meditating on these two concepts that I had gleaned from my parents in my early years, and it was in that state of mind that my OT session ended, and my PT session began. As I mentally prepared for the next workout, I remembered that I was officially starting my regular sessions with Kim as my physical therapist.

VISIONS AND DREAMS

Sandra handed me off to my new therapist, and said goodbye for the day.

"Hi, Roland! How's your day going?" Kim was her usual cheery self.

Fresh off my meditative cloud, I was happy to see her. "I'm good! Ready for a change of pace." My head was clear, and I was open to anything.

"First of all, I really do want to talk to you about websites, and I brought you my card, so you have my number, and I want yours as well." I gave her my phone number, which she scribbled on a small piece of paper, and I managed to wriggle her card into the pocket of my gym shorts. She placed the piece of paper in the pocket of her scrubs-like uniform, and placed both of her hands on her hips like Wonder Woman.

"Okay. We're going to start with something you may not have done yet." That got my instant full attention. "It's called visualization." She was pushing my wheelchair across the room, out the door to who knew where, and I was captivated. Down some hallways and a couple of turns later, and we were in the garden that I'd heard her describing to the cancer patient with the sourpuss attitude.

"Ah, I remember you telling that one lady last week about this garden, the one with cancer." I wanted to ask about that patient. I wondered how she was dealing with a person who seemed to have a very good reason to be negative and grouchy. "How's she doing anyway? It seems that your job can be very difficult at times."

"YES! That first day was especially like that, but you should see her now! She's getting around, talking to everybody, and even planning a wedding shower for another patient who is getting married." It was quite a remarkable report. I wondered if we could possibly be talking about the same lady.

"Is that right? What a trip..." My thinking was short circuited for

ROLAND'S STORY

a minute while I tried to picture the grouchy lady transformed in a few short weeks to a joyous party planner.

"Yes! Isn't that something? Okay now, let's get you going." Kim rolled me to a corner of the garden, away from the doors and windows of the facility, and I was at once transported to a different world. Trees, rose bushes, loads of greenery, flowers of all kinds and, of course, a fountain being used as a bath by a couple of sparrows.

"Wow." I said. "What a change." We hung out for a few minutes and enjoyed the garden, the smells and colors filling me with dynamic input.

"Now, I want you to take some deep breaths, and relax... sit up straight, but try not to be tense." It was easy. I felt like I was on a vacation from the world in which I'd been imprisoned for two months.

"Now, close your eyes, and imagine yourself in the garden as you really are, but you can see yourself. In your mind, you are looking out your eyes, and down on your body, and you are sitting normally on a bench or in a chair... hands are in your lap... feet, flat on the ground..." In my mind I was sitting on that bench, relaxed, and could imagine the garden wrapped around me, with its color and lush leaves.

"Now, see yourself rise from your chair, and take a few steps towards the flowers and trees..." I saw the world accept my choice to stand, allowing me to step slowly, deliberately, moving on the concrete that curved through the garden. I even imagined seeing a lizard scurry across the cement, and rush off into the tall grasses of some plants.

"Reach out, Roland... reach out and touch the leaves of a plant or a tree... you choose. Use your right hand." I felt the sun shining on me. I felt the breeze. It made the rest easy to create in my mind.

VISIONS AND DREAMS

I was reaching using my right arm, and my fingers were slowly closing to gently feel a small cluster of leaves.

"Now look around you, Roland, and take in all the beauty as you make your way back to your spot on the bench. Go ahead and sit again. Take a couple more deep breaths... take it all in." It was like a dream. But something I was in control of. My experience was my choice. It was surrealistic, yet everything looked to me as my brain commanded.

"Okay, now close your eyes." It was a puzzling request. It gave my visualization a jolt. I was caught up in two sensations of reality. In one, I was sitting in my wheelchair in a garden with my eyes already closed. In the other, I was on a bench, sitting in a similar garden, about to close my eyes to what I was envisioning. They seemed to blend for a moment in surrealistic reality, with the smells and physical sensations of sun and wind giving life to my vision. And as I saw the little microcosm before me in the world that I had assembled in my mind, I slowly closed my mind to the vision.

There was silence for a minute or so. Then Kim spoke again. "How're you feeling?"

"Good. No, I feel great! It was like dreaming. Only I was in charge." I was still absorbing the significance of what just happened.

"It's called visual motor rehearsal. They use it with astronauts and athletes. The mind literally can't tell the difference between doing it and thinking it." She was pushing me conceptually, and she knew it. "There is a philosophy called the Law of Attraction, and it promotes the concept that we create our own reality. By what you're thinking, the Universe responds, and..."

"Wait a minute - stop." I held my hand up like a crossing guard. "What did you just say?"

So she started all over again, and I lowered my hand. When she got to "reality" again, my hand flew up again and she immediate paused.

"That's what I thought you said: we create our own reality. My dad used to tell me that all the time over forty years ago. I want to hear more. What was that philosophy called again?"

"The Law of Attraction. But we should get cracking on your workout while we've still got some time left. Say goodbye, garden!" I actually replied verbally to our garden and my surrealistic vision, and reluctantly agreed to Kim rolling us back into the facility, down some hallways and some turns, and emerged back in the workout room amidst the menagerie.

Kim had me standing with the help of a walker and the borrowed ankle-foot orthosis (AFO), applying a limited support by hand to my knee. In my mind's eye, I linked together the concepts of standing there and walking in the garden, and could picture the two stages near enough to each other that the walk in the garden was suddenly reachable, and just a small leap in concepts. It really didn't look as far away as I had thought.

Kim promised we'd talk again. I found myself thinking about how I might improve my rehab progress by incorporating more visualizations. She had called it "visual motor rehearsal." I was going to find myself busy researching visualization, and that philosophy called the Law of Attraction.

That evening, I told Barbara about everything that had happened that day. She smiled as I talked, seeing me excited about rehab for the first time since the stroke. She was thrilled with me. We discussed giving Kim an introduction to the web, the visualization idea, and the way Kim had repeated my dad's words when only a half hour before I had been meditating on those exact words.

"There's something to this. I don't believe in chance, and I know you don't either." I said. "I've got her card now, so we can even call her sometime."

"That's a great idea. Wait, she wants a website?" Barbara broke into a big smile. "Ha hah!" She threw her head back and laughed as I nodded my head in a slow, animated affirmative. It was a standing joke that I often negotiated a trade out with clients needing a website if they had services or products of which we were in need.

That night, as opposed to watching TV, I was researching concepts that I had been introduced to by Kim. My mind was swimming in ideas, and what I found was that reading about these things wasn't like learning something new. I felt like I'd known the principle of visual motor rehearsal, and had been doing something like it for years.

Then I found some excerpts from books that were ringing bells in the archives of my mind. How could I know this stuff without ever having seen the material? My mind was draw-stringing things together. A pattern was forming. I felt like I was Sherlock Holmes, about to solve the great mystery.

Earl Nightingale was famous for the line, "We become what we think about."

Buddha spread his message, "We are what we think. All that we are arises with our thoughts"

In researching the Law of Attraction, something was taking definite shape, and reinforcing everything else I had learned that made sense to me. The basic premise was that "that which is like unto itself is drawn." I was ready to believe in the concept, and could see attracting good things, bad things, according to your thinking, but it still didn't explain my stroke. Surely I hadn't through conscious thought brought this stroke to myself. Somewhere, there was a link missing in the chain of truth.

It must have been close to three o'clock in the morning. Something had started that day in the garden that needed to be finished. My dad's words echoed over and over… "We create our own reality." I was talking to myself, probably out loud.

"So, if we created our reality, and Earl and Buddha were right, then it follows that when we envision peace, love, and harmony then we're attracting that in our lives. And my mom says that the spiritual precedes the physical, and the spirit is consciousness, then our thoughts are the beginning of the spiritual changing the physical, because we become what we think about…"

The mathematical logistician in me was hard at work on elements that were not traditionally quantifiable, and equations that no one had ever shown me. "And if we worry, that doesn't serve us, because we cause ourselves more worry. And if we argue and fight, that obviously causes more of the same. And Jesus told us to 'love thine enemies', so that made sense, break the cycle…"

I was reading articles and watching videos online that were suddenly bringing everything that I had been studying all my life into focus. The more I learned, the more I realized there was truth being repeated throughout thousands of years. When you boiled it down, it was using different terms, but telling the same truths.

I kept on pushing, feeling that something was about to give way.

"So, if we hold onto good, happy thoughts, then we're attracting more of that. And by fearing things in life and worrying, we're getting out of synchronization with the Universe, and slowing down the natural energy of healing and abundance causing stress and high blood pressure and things like strokes, and… wait a minute."

I was beginning to get a clear picture of the Law of Cause and Effect, Buddha principles, the Law of Attraction, and mom's words and dad's insights pulling together into one dynamic bundle. The room was dark, other than the light from my laptop. I sat upright in

VISIONS AND DREAMS

bed, the table extended across my lap with my computer. It was like standing on the edge of a cliff, with old logic telling me I would fall, and new logic, using principles like the ones I'd been reviewing for hours now, telling me that it was not so. The new logic was telling me that just because it looked like I'd fall did not mean that was the only possibility.

As I lay there, staring into the computer screen, my thoughts blotting out any recognition of the subject matter, I realized how extremely tired I felt. My brain was overloading with the data from the computer. I decided to close my eyes to try and rest them from the contrast of images and text hammering them, and I began a lucid move into a dream state.

The odd thing was, I wasn't really dreaming. Or was I? As far as I was concerned all I had done was close my eyes. My mind made no such transition that usually accompanied falling asleep. Just as I had been visualizing in the garden with my eyes closed, I was doing the same thing now. Only I wasn't in the garden… I was standing on the edge of a cliff.

As I analyzed what was happening in this state, I started testing the ability of my mind to conduct the scene that I was experiencing. I felt light, and being in a standing position, that meant that my imagination was already engaged, holding my world together in a reality separate from my usual waking state.

How could I be asleep and yet so in control of my thoughts and experience? Usually in a dream, it was all a matter of reacting to odd circumstances, and watching, like it was a movie. Where I was right now, I was the conductor of a sci-fi play with an interactive plot.

I decided to fly.

Extending my arms, I floated off the cliff's edge, and curved through empty space, not actually floating off the cliff, but curving back toward solid ground, and directing myself toward some modern looking buildings not far away. The fear of falling gone, I knew that I need not fear anything. I flew the distance easily, feeling only a light breeze like I had in the garden. Approaching a building, my body pivoted so that my legs came back under me and I floated to an impact free landing.

As easily as I had taken flight, I found myself walking into the building. High tech and amazingly clean, free of dirt, trash, or anything like what we'd find in a building on any downtown street, I took a few steps, and examined my surroundings. I hadn't created the building on purpose, it was just there. A few people were making their way, no one rushing. A tall man was walking toward me. He was dressed sharply in a suit that expressed style, class and sensibility, matching his persona of quality and confidence. As he came close, his walking slowed, and he stopped a couple yards away, no intention obvious. His face was serene. He needed nothing from me, but he was devoted to the moment, returning my gaze.

"I know that I'm dreaming this." I said to the man. He merely maintained his casual stance, and slowly nodded his head in acknowledgment, letting me know that he was apparently aware of my purpose, even if I was not.

"I mean I know I am here, standing in my dream, talking to you." The man nodded again, tipping his head slightly, as if to say, "Also true." There was no pressure to say more.

The man in the suit merely stood there as if to confirm my participation in this exquisite dream, and connect with me, so that I wasn't just an observer of the magnificent place that I was visiting, but had been accounted for by another presence. He was too real and vital to be just my imagination. At once I had the distinct feeling that he was as real as I was, creating a body that was whole, and

VISIONS AND DREAMS

flying like a superman. So this person from somewhere was creating something of his own for me to see that was real too.

Everything faded to gray over the next few seconds, and suddenly I was back in my bed and body, staring at my computer screen. It was blank. That meant my laptop had gone to sleep mode, which takes ten minutes of non-action to do. I'd been motionless for that long.

Yet I wasn't stiff, sleepy, or anything related to having been dreaming. My head wasn't hanging forward on my chest. I had perfect clarity, as if I had been having a wakeful conversation with someone who had spent time with me, and just blinked my eyes, and then he, and the others, decided to go their way, and they dissolved into another dimension...

...Or, maybe that had been me.

19

LIVING PROOF

It had taken me another half hour to disengage from the whole study-dream experience, and finally fall into a dreamless sleep for a few hours. I maintained a complete recall of my experience, and was still processing it as I went about the usual morning activities of using the toilet, washing up, and preparing for breakfast.

I turned the TV on with the volume low, and eventually switched it off. I sat there thinking about the dream I'd had, if it was a dream, and was surprised to note that every aspect of what I originally experienced was still within my waking memory. I could remember every detail like replaying a movie. Just before breakfast, I came to a conclusion that gave me an eerie feeling, and raised the hairs on the back of my neck, not out of fear, but excitement.

I couldn't wait to tell Barbara, and when I called her at work, she was unprepared to digest what I was saying to her. Although she wanted to be attentive, and well aware that I had undergone something important, she had the running of a large retail store on her mind, and mornings were always demanding for management. Realizing that my timing was poor, I let her go, saying that I'd give

LIVING PROOF

her more of the details later when she came to join me at the center after work.

Breakfast was uneventful, and I shoved my table out of the way. Calling for a CAN, I got help changing to workout clothes, and getting in the wheelchair. Not so patiently, I waited for Sandra to arrive. As usual, mid-morning she was there to start my day of therapy.

On the way to the workout room we passed by a doorway, and I recognized Jean, the "Match.com Mama," and she was talking feverishly, and propelling herself in her chair, her eyes upon things hanging from her wall. I begged Sandra to stop and roll back until I could see Jean.

"Morning, Jean! What's going on?" Responding to her name, she looked up and smiled, wild-eyed and excited.

"Hi, Roland! How ya doin'? Oh, I am so excited..." she was on fire.

"I can tell." I interjected as she continued on her way. I noticed a huge bruise around her left eye, and was going to ask about it, but never got the chance.

"You know Kim, my therapist, right, she's gonna help me write some children's books, and I have all these ideas, and her son's gonna draw my characters..." She wasn't in the mood to use periods, so she just blazed on. "... these are some of his drawings, and he's good, so I have a story about a baby elephant, and one about 'BK,' the child of Batman and Cat Woman, and these are some prototypes..."

Jean could switch topics and not miss a beat, and still not use a period. "...you know I was really down the other day, so I asked her, 'Kim,' I said, 'would you want live if you were in my situation,' and you know what she said, she told me that the world needs me and my sense of humor, ha ha, and my love, compassion, and my faith, and made me realize that I have something to give. And that as long as we are breathing we have work to do, and she said, 'after all, we're here for a reason,' so I'm going to start writing, and these pictures are making me excited and giving me more and more ideas..."

I knew I had to move away, and was trying to be polite. "... and you know, that Kim, well she is so sweet, and I just love her to bits, because she has like given me a reason to live, cuz I was starting to wonder 'what the heck,' you know." She paused for the first time in several minutes, and looked at Sandra and me. I grabbed the moment to excuse Sandra and myself so we could stay on schedule.

Jean continued on, relentlessly. "... so, anyway, just wanted to tell you about my books, and this picture here... you know, I think that I like this one better, so I'll do that story first..." She continued rambling as we rolled down the hall, and I wondered if there was actually someone in the room listening to her that we hadn't seen. As we reached the limits of hearing range, she was still going. "...and she said, 'Oh my God, your eye,' and I said, 'You should see the OTHER guy,' ha ha..."

"Wow!" I said to Sandra.

"Yeah. Wow is right!" Sandra reinforced. "I'd say she is a little excited."

We went along the hall to the workout room. The therapy administration office was a small cubicle near the workout room, and as we passed, the door being ajar, we were able to hear a conversation in progress, not meant to be public.

"...it's the same thing again. You're always getting too involved with the patients. And this book writing nonsense. It's another example of you sticking your nose where it doesn't belong." The supervisor was apparently addressing a subject that could only be regarding Jean's new projects.

"But I thought it was important that she feels inspired and..." We were beyond hearing range, and the noise of the workout room obliterated any overtones of voices from the office. It was obvious that Kim was the target of the administrator's speech, and it sounded like she was being reprimanded. It hardly made sense. From what I had witnessed, the administration should be awarding her a medal, and stylizing their entire therapy program based on what she was doing.

A few minutes later, Kim was slowly wheeling her patient in for therapy. She was hesitating just inside the doorway, and I could hear her trying to speak quietly. "Do you want to go back to your room for a bit? We don't have to do this now, Rebecca." So that was her name. No longer a grouch, I had heard that in spite of her condition, she was cheerful, her pain had magically disappeared, and she was apparently walking short distances on her own. They had started calling her by the nickname, "Butterfly," because of her complete metamorphosis from a crab apple, to a sweet, loving person.

"No, it's fine, Kim. I just can't believe it. When I went to the oncologist for my checkup just now, I expected him to tell me that I had a month or so to live." Kim glanced around, as if to inspect the potential audience that the conversation might be inadvertently catering to. I kept my eyes forward as Sandra attached E-stim tabs to my arm. But I heard every word, and couldn't stop myself from listening. "The cancer is gone. There wasn't a trace of it on the x-ray!"

A few heads turned, mostly therapists, who were used to catching technical terminology in their everyday work dialogues. The room lost a lot of ambient noise as several conversations halted abruptly.

"You know, when I thought I was going to die, I gave away everything I had. I let go of my home, my belongings, and all my money." She had been wiping tears away. Seeming to recover, she cocked her head to one side and appeared thoughtful.

I think my healing began at that point, when I released my attachments to all things and all people. There, inside that release grew the seed that healed me, my untethered connection to God. Oh, that and physical therapy!"

With that, Rebecca was hugging Kim, and their verbal exchange was more intimate. I'd been so involved with what Rebecca was saying, that I had unconsciously turned to blatantly become a committed spectator, as had everyone else in the room. It was as if the emotions being held at bay were tipping over the damn.

"Congratulations, Rebecca!" said someone.

"Yeah, way to go!" added another.

People began clapping their hands. More people were joining in the cheering and shouting their congratulations. The room was in uproar, with therapists leaving their charges to sit by themselves as they hustled across the room and lined up to add their arms to the bundle that was Rebecca, Kim, and a growing mass of devoted fans.

I saw the administrator pause in the doorway, observing. His stone face displayed disapproval, but who cared. Kim was doing the right thing. Therapy was more than putting in time and going through the motions, and someday they'd be asking Kim to teach them how to find unique solutions, instead of telling her to get back in line.

For me, this represented something more. The count was three. This was the third time that applause and cheering had rocked the workout room. A table will stand on three legs. Three's a charm. One-two-three-go! It was my unavoidable conclusion that this was a confirmation that Kim was inextricably connected to the events going on that had steadily progressed from inspiring, to magical, to impossible. That which had been notoriously demonic as an adversary, cancer, had been abolished today, and no one could deny the miraculous nature of the historic event.

This knowledge that cancer had been conquered, at least for one little lady who had been condemned to death, was the final stage of converting me to a believer. From now on, no one could tell me that there wasn't a chance of me walking again. However long it took, I knew that success awaited me as long I didn't give up.

I saw the significance of the personal transformation that had taken place in Rebecca, and how the change of spirit had healed her. "The spiritual precedes the physical," my mom used to say. And, "We create our own reality," were dad's words. Everything I had learned since I was a kid that I held as truths was now allowed to take a final hold inside me.

I now understood the difference between the concept of faith and having faith. Until you were unalterably convinced, and no one could sway you, faith would remain a concept, balanced against shadows of doubt that caused fear, resentment, and anger. I was a witness to the transformation. If Rebecca could be cured of cancer, I was unalterably convinced, finally, after more than two months, that I would be achieving wholeness again. My doubt was gone, and with it went any remnants of lingering fear, resentment, or anger.

We spent the rest of the therapy hour working on a cycle, but with my hands attached to the machine as well, trying to give my arm some much needed motion.

Kim was in charge of my next session, but having been overwhelmed as we all were from Rebecca's announcement of the disappearance of all traces of her cancer, the patients and therapists were all talking, slow to engage in anything requiring too much concentration. Mostly we executed partial workouts, bookended with discussions regarding what had happened, and the unbelievable miracle of complete recovery from certain doom.

I didn't hammer Kim with questions, or blurt out the revelations that had occurred both in her presence and by myself. I was sure that we'd have time to pursue the subject of healing further aside

ROLAND'S STORY

from the environment of the rehab workout room. I asked her to come by my room later so we could talk. Kim agreed.

As she rolled me back to my room, we were both feeling like we'd been inhaling through oxygen masks in a world with toxic air. She bounced out of the room and headed on to her next subject.

20

SHOCK AND DISAPPOINTMENT

That was the last time I'd see Kim while in the Lynfield Rehab Center.

What no one knew was that as she ended her workday, the administrator called her into his office to announce that they had decided to let her go. The vague excuses revolved around excessive patient interaction, not following traditional protocols, and assisting patients in getting the help they needed by counseling them on their insurance options and care for which they qualified, but for whatever reasons, were not being presented as options.

No write up. No exit interview to go over their concerns or her intentions. No warning. He just let her go on the spot. After seven years of employment, even a bad employee would have expected more.

The ridiculousness of the situation was appalling. The objective of a rehab was to encourage healing, or at least to provide comfort. One therapist out of many was finding multiple ways of accomplishing this, and they had fired her. Every rehab patient was different. Hence, it made sense if you applied similar formulas to all, you'd have varying degrees of success, and more likelihood of missing the target for developing the best means of finding any success at all.

As we had witnessed, even someone with a terminal illness could reverse their death march. It may have nothing to do with the therapy, and everything to do with the caring ministrations of a physical therapist, daring to act like a human being while directed to be a robot.

No one was told that Kim had been fired. The word being passed around was she'd quit. I had been picked up by Irene as I had been for weeks, and she indicated that Kim had suddenly quit the day before. I kept silent, but I was certain that there was more to the story.

Rebecca was outraged. She was sure Kim had not left on her own account. Kim wouldn't leave us like that. In order for her not to live in negativity, she began working out her plan on how to exit the establishment that had vanquished her hero.

The Teddy Bear returned to his loud, belligerent self, and once again, nurses and assistants were steering clear, gossiping in the hall outside his door.

Jean was devastated. Her dream of writing children's books died an early death, and her vivacious, talkative personality was replaced with a quiet, dark depression.

Barbara was livid. She had not met Kim yet, but had listened to me talk about my new therapist and the things she was doing. Here I was, excited for the first time in months, and the lady responsible was gone? We discussed the situation, and concluded there was much more to it.

I had Kim's number. I was the only one not too concerned. I wasn't aware of all the facts at the time. But I was okay. It was probably from my recent changes in thinking that I wasn't even worried for Kim's sake. I had heard the administrator's speech. If doing what she was good at and helping people heal wasn't appropriate for a

SHOCK AND DISAPPOINTMENT

medical rehab facility and nursing home, then it was the wrong place for her. Unfortunately, many patients were going to be affected by her absence.

And as for me, I had her number.

Two things were happening that would positively enhance my life. First, Stacy had found a company that would develop a knee brace and an AFO specifically designed to fit my right leg. A rep from the company was scheduled the next day to take a casting of my leg. The second thing was that Stacy had located an acute rehab that agreed to accept me as a patient. I could transfer in the next few days.

Either way, I had Kim's number. I knew that I would find a way to benefit from her knowledge and skill. I had no idea what magic she brought with her, but I knew it was there. I was simply going to call her and work it out.

With everyone reacting in a number of ways, I was oddly serene. One person had left the establishment, but it was interesting how so many people were affected so negatively. I was concerned for Kim's sake. After all, she was probably unemployed now.

Well, I'd be in touch with her. Meanwhile, I had new adventures to attend to.

PART III
Transformation

21

THREE IS NOT ALWAYS A CHARM

I admit that in spite of the fact of Kim leaving Lynfield, regardless of circumstances, I was already benefiting from the brief period when she was my PT. I was using the visualization process she taught me every day. Plus, I knew anything was possible.

Knowing that I was going to get better was a given. More importantly, since I was aware of how I was responsible for my condition by previously creating poorly with fear, doubt, and worry, the only logical conclusion was I also had the power to fix it with confidence, peacefulness and faith. As a matter of fact, I knew I was the only one who could.

A few days later, Stacy announced that my AFO and leg brace were ready, and would be delivered the next day. Also, in the afternoon, Tustin Acute Rehabilitation Hospital would call and let me know when my room was ready. It appeared that everything in my world was starting to synchronize.

ROLAND'S STORY

There was to be no ambulance ride this time. Barbara would be driving me to Tustin herself. With the exceptions of the facility being newer, bigger, and each bed came equipped with its own mini-TV on an adjustable arm that played programs inches from the patient's face, Tustin turned out to be another corporate controlled rehab. The biggest difference in being there was that it was specifically a rehab facility. No one was there biding their time until a disease or old age took them away.

Once I'd transferred from Lynfield, I did miss certain people and staff members. I carried fond memories of a World War II veteran and his made up words of the Marine's Hymn. I laughed to think of characters shouting out things like, "You shut up!" and "Put me back in there!" My days in the menagerie were over. I wondered how I had managed to hang on to my sanity. I had made friends with therapists and patients, many of whom I would never see again.

Now I was at the final level of my hospitalized rehab program before going home. It was supposed to ensure that when I finally was released from hospital care entirely, I could fend for myself. Or at least do so with limited assistance from Barbara. I had confidence that I could manage well enough. What I hoped to gain was some last tips on building myself up and better tactics for learning to stand and walk.

I still had very little going on in my right arm or leg, and needed to wake up the parts of my body that had been lying dormant for months. At least I was no longer looking for a miracle worker to touch me with a magic wand. My plan was to keep positive, and know that eventually I'd be there.

I was getting good at this. By the day after my arrival, I had my meals arranged, therapy scheduled and internet connected.

THREE IS NOT ALWAYS A CHARM

But being organized didn't keep mediocre attitudes in my environment inhibiting my energy flow. I still had a long way to go in creating reality the way I wanted it.

The style of initiation of Lynfield repeated itself in Tustin, with the OT, PT, and Speech Therapist spending the first day evaluating my condition. I had no issues with speech, and the therapist and I ended up having a very pleasant conversation. However, the PT and OT were something of a different challenge than what I'd experienced at Lynfield. They both had a commanding air about them, and led me to believe that they had skills and abilities that would outshine my previous therapists, and maybe leave me with better practical tools for recovery.

I had developed a speech for delivery to the therapists that would be working on me physically, and delivered it twice with what I believed was clarity of purpose. Each time, to the PT and then the OT, I believed I had left no question regarding my expectations.

"I don't believe for a second that you will have me walking out of here in two weeks. But I do think that you can teach me exercises that will help me strengthen muscles, and wake up my limbs so that when I leave here I can continue to help myself."

It was my new level of self-confidence, and an early exercise in creating my own reality. I was realizing that in order to get better, I had to see myself well and whole, and expect it. But in conjunction with what I'd seen of rehab staff, and seeing as though I was in their care for these two weeks, their contribution to my rehabilitation still fell in the realm of questionable. If they turned out to be like Kim, my attitude was ready to change accordingly.

As it turned out, my practiced speech was ignored, and each therapist launched into a battle plan of their own, leaving me doubtful that my wishes and expectations had been registered.

ROLAND'S STORY

Other than just getting through my two weeks, all I wanted was to be left alone. I was close to going home now, and I needed no more exciting events unless they involved healing. I wanted to spend my time further educating myself in spiritual studies and mind development, so I could gain as much advantage as possible in learning self-healing.

Barbara continued to visit me daily after work, which was much harder now that I was almost thirty miles from home, and the only way to get to me was by impacted freeways and longer, slower side roads.

The advantages of Lynfield that I forfeited were mostly that the nurses, assistants and therapists knew me, and knew what I needed regarding my temporary living space. As if to demonstrate the contrast, that night a new CNA came on duty, and he was immediately busy with his duties. Hector took one look at my arrangement of laptop, books, and documents and achieved an attitude in three seconds flat. He charged around performing his duties of changing sheets, cleaning, and arranging, and in the process left me out of reach of my urinal, misplaced my tissue box, and positioned my call control so that the moment I touched it, the connector came unplugged from the wall, and immediately the beeper went off like I'd called for help.

Oh, Lord, I thought. Of course, the first to respond was Hector.

"What do you need?" He demanded, as he stalked in to see what the problem was.

"Well, the call control was barely in the wall, and as soon as I... " Without waiting to hear the end of my sentence, he went off.

"You know, it's all this stuff! I can't work like this! These cables are supposed to be a certain way..." He kept at it for a minute, apparently having plenty of opinion to express on the subject. I wondered who had made his day so perfect that he felt inclined to share it with me.

THREE IS NOT ALWAYS A CHARM

"You know, there's no place for your toys here. I can't work with all this..." I guess I was still learning the way of the peaceful warrior, for I felt myself start to bristle.

"Wait a minute - that is not a toy, it's a two-thousand dollar laptop, and I use it to conduct my business..." It was the start of a true statement, although for most of two months I'd used it mostly to send emails and watch Netflix.

"These kind of toys have no place here. This is a hospital, and there's no room for this stuff." He charged on, and I let him. Obviously, he was not about to listen to any debate, and had made up his mind regarding the value of my laptop. When he was finally done and gone, I took my time disconnecting, reconnecting, and rearranging my paraphernalia so that whether I was in my wheelchair or the bed, I could easily reach everything.

Later that evening, the nurse, a wonderful lady named Miriam, came in to give me my meds. I greeted her, and asked if we could speak.

"Yes. What can I help you with?" She was so pleasant that I almost didn't want to express what amounted to my first real complaint regarding the personnel in three facilities.

"It's not like me to complain, as I'm pretty congenial..." I started to back off, but then remembered how Hector had rudely interrupted me and ignored what I was trying to say. "Basically, if that guy Hector is going to be allowed the attitude that he came in here with today, I don't want him touching me, my things, my bed, not even my urinal."

"Oh, my," said Miriam. "What did he do?"

I gave her a version of the event minus my reaction, which I hadn't actually expressed to him on the spot, but wanted to. She was sincerely concerned, and said she would have a word with him.

"You don't have to do that, necessarily." I was trying not to let myself get too agitated. "But I just wanted you to know that if he hands me any more of that, even the smallest bit of sarcasm or anything, I'm going to stand up on my own for the first time since my stroke, and throw him out of here myself." Once I got going I was not in a mind to pull punches, and I felt myself heating. "But, I mean, well, you know, I can't accept disrespect from someone who doesn't even know me."

Miriam remained cool and collected. She explained it was the assistant's job to make sure we were comfortable, helping us with things like setting up our laptops, or games, or anything that would make our stay a little easier.

"That's what I thought." I thought silently, and probably displayed to Miriam a face of mild bewilderment.

Satisfied that I'd appropriately represented the incident and expressed my intentions, I let Miriam go to take care of the rest of her patients. My night went without incident after our discussion. I did my research for the evening until I was bleary eyed, finally letting my laptop, and myself, go to sleep mode.

The next morning, I awakened to a hustling CNA busily taking care of morning duties. As Hector walked by, he grabbed my urinal and walked away with it, even though I had not used it since the last cleaning. When he returned from the bathroom, there was no urinal, and he headed out the door. He hadn't made it three steps, and I was on my call button.

"What do you want?" He said, returning to the room, obviously irritated.

"I want my urinal, and I want it right now!" This was the first time I'd had to ask for it, and I was immediately on guard.

"No, you're supposed to use the john, and it's good for you to practice standing." That does it, I thought. This guy was not my nurse or my therapist. As often as I had to use the urinal, I wasn't going to start trying to "hold it" as I waited for someone to help

THREE IS NOT ALWAYS A CHARM

me into a wheelchair, hustle me into the bathroom, repack me into a chair, and make the transfer back to bed, every time I had to go.

"Stop! Go get me my urinal right now, or I'll make sure someone else does. As a matter of fact, forget it. You can go now. Just leave. And don't you answer the call from my button!"

I'd had it. It was hard to admit that I was losing it. Hector, flustered at my outburst, turned and walked out. Several minutes later, Miriam came in and knowingly nodded her head.

"I heard," she said. "What Hector didn't tell you is that the head of therapy, Pablo, told him to do that."

"It would have gone a lot easier if he had explained that." So, the issue was deeper than just a senseless assistant. There seemed to be a definite communication issue. She retrieved my urinal and assured me that she'd handle the situation.

Later, a very sheepish Hector came in doing the next round of chores. He made it a point to be pleasant, saying things like, "Can I get you anything else?" and "Would you like some fresh water?"

I was puzzled. Henceforth, I didn't have to worry about my things being moved or my urinal missing. But there was a pattern to what was happening that I didn't like.

22

DAILY FAILURE TO COMMUNICATE

Therapy was therapy. I still wasn't learning how to build up my muscle strength, and I wasn't any closer to walking than I was at Lynfield. The weird thing was the communication issues were going to continue, and become a trademark of the Tustin Rehab.

A couple days later, Pablo himself was working with me, and was able to see the incredible amount of tone that afflicted my right arm. He suggested that a muscle relaxer might be helpful. I didn't agree or disagree. It didn't sound like an order or even a suggestion. So that night, when the nurse mentioned a certain drug had been prescribed for me for "muscle spasms," I protested.

"No, that can't be for me. I'm not having muscle spasms." As far as I was concerned, a muscle spasm was a sudden and involuntary contraction, like a cramp.

THREE IS NOT ALWAYS A CHARM

"That's what it says here. Muscle spasms. It's optional." The nurse on duty said. "You don't have to take it."

I declined. I wasn't at all sure that the drug was meant for me, and they had me taking enough medications as it was. I really didn't want to add to them. She withheld the spasm drug, and left me wondering how there could be any confusion regarding medications in such a well-acclaimed hospital.

The next day at therapy, Pablo approached me and asked, "I heard you refused the muscle relaxer last night. Why?"

I was seriously bugged by now. "Pablo, did you order that muscle relaxer for me?"

"Yes." He replied. "Remember, we talked about it?"

"We talked about the tone in my arm, yes." I said. "But the medicine was prescribed for muscle spasms. You never referred to my arm as having spasms."

"Yeah..." Pablo looked at the floor. "We use that drug for tone issues. Sometimes we refer to it as spasms."

"Well, don't you think you could have explained the terminology to me? And maybe alerted me that you had prescribed anything at all? I was sure they were giving me someone else's medication, because you didn't make it clear."

He apologized, and we let it drop. The whole thing left a bad taste in my mouth. All in all, I couldn't wait to leave Tustin. The mere fact that every day had been a miscommunication of some sort had me troubled. Three more days did not change my opinion of the hospital.

What I knew was that no one was listening to my request to help me get strong. The therapy department insisted in making me stand on a leg that I couldn't even lift off the bed, let alone move in a stepping action. They concentrated on my leg, and did little with my arm.

It seemed like their attitude was, "Since your arm is lame, we'll show you how to make the best of it, so you can function better." I didn't want to just live with it. I wanted to get my arm, and my leg working again. It became obvious that I wasn't going to get what I wanted.

I decided that it was time to call Kim.

23

ENGAGING IN A NEW OUTLOOK

Just making the decision to call Kim made me feel better.

I was still practicing my visualization technique, and expanding to more imagined processes. I pictured swinging a racquet in a racquetball court. I did karate moves in my mind, and imagined the slow motion Tai Chi-like gesture of my right hand sweeping through the air. I even played a song on my guitar that I loved, hearing every note sing like I was Carlos Santana.

These visions weren't totally imaginary. A few short months ago, I'd been doing them all. My mind remembered how. I just had to remind my hand and arm.

Late one morning, just before lunch, I located Kim's card, laboriously attached my wired earpiece so I could be "hand-free," and gave her a call.

"Hello?" She answered on the third ring.

"Hi, Kim. This is Roland, from Lynfield Rehab." I knew she would know me with that description, yet hated to bring up bad memories.

"Oh, hello, Roland. How are you?" She sounded a bit subdued

from her usual vibrant self. But that made sense, under the circumstances.

"Kim, I need your help. I want to get well, and I know I will. I believe you're my ticket." The time for pleasantries was over.

"Well, I'm flattered. Thanks for thinking of me. I guess I've got time now, because I'm unemployed." Kim wasn't as bitter as I thought she'd be. But she did sound a bit lost.

We talked for a while. My lunch came, and I ignored it. An hour later we were still talking. I told her about the patients who were missing her in Lynfield. I told her about the lies being generated regarding her supposed resignation. I told her about my disturbing experiences in the Tustin rehab.

"I tell you what, Kim." I had a great idea, and was in a perfect position to help her. "Let's do a trade out. You help me work on getting my arm and leg stronger, and I'll build you a website, with a blog, a video and picture gallery, and design it so you can sell your services online."

"Really?" She was surprised at the offer. "I'll be glad to help you, Roland. But a website is expensive. I can't ask you to do that."

"You're not asking. I'm offering. It's not as expensive as you think." I assured her. "We both need some help right now. I've been to three supposedly great healthcare institutions, and not one of them has really been able to help me. If you help me get well, and I know you can do that, I will build your site, host it for you, teach you how to blog, teach you how to upload your own photos and videos, and install a shopping cart so you can sell services, a workout video series, and t-shirts, and it'll drop the money right into your bank account."

There was silence on the other end of the phone. I heard a bit of a sniffle. "Roland, I really don't know what to say."

"How about 'Yes!' And if you want to add a thank you to that, you

ENGAGING IN A NEW OUTLOOK

can. But by God, you don't owe me more than I owe you, Kim. So we'll consider it a fair trade. You showed me a way of healing that I believe works when a dozen therapists, and three teams of nurses and doctors could not."

I found myself having a laugh spasm, the kind of spasm that I WAS familiar with, but minus the laugh. For a few seconds, I couldn't catch my breath, and I certainly couldn't talk. I wondered if Pablo's prescription for muscle spasms could help me with this.

"Okay, yes!" She waited for me to say something more, and several seconds passed. "Roland?" Kim ventured. "Are you okay?"

"Yeah, Kim." I wheezed. I was recovering, and caught between the urges and laughing and crying, and I was having trouble summoning enough control to speak. I was feeling happier than I had for months. Kim patiently waited.

I reached with my left hand, and took my right, and twisted it palm up. As I looked at my hands, I suddenly had the urge to imagine the right one opening and closing, like in the visualization exercises that Kim had taught me. Just then my index finger jumped just a bit, and then my thumb followed. My heart leaped. They hadn't moved independently since the stroke. Mesmerized at my own fingers, I tried moving them, first my index finger, then my thumb. On command, they responded until I was convinced of what I was witnessing. I knew that with Kim's encouragement, I had taken back a part of my body, and that, rehabs be damned, I could do it myself... maybe with a little help from Kim and Barbara.

I managed to calm myself enough to say what was on my mind. I'd been saying it from the start, but now, it had a meaning that was unique for me, enhanced by nearly three months in rehab, self-discovery, and all the experiences that the stroke had brought.

"You know, Kim, I really am in good hands after all."

EPILOGUE

SIX MONTHS LATER...

In Southern California, we're spoiled by good weather. For a brief time, fall brings earth-tone colors to Orange County, the leaves fall, and flowers temporarily dwindle. Highly efficient crews of landscapers armed with gas powered blowers round up the leaves, trim the branches, and shape the hedges, maintaining the uniformity of our collaborative designs.

I remember my first winter, with temperatures of sixty to seventy degrees during the day, sunshine and clear skies. Often, wispy cirrus clouds accented the sunsets in their glorious arrays of fiery golds, impossible blues, pinks, and purples that artists use for their inspirations, yet fall short in their attempts to represent the true glory of nature's expression.

I watched the barely discernible flight of clouds, knowing that as the earth performed its continuous pirouette, the sun would appear to approach the horizon, deepening the hues, and the amazing display that is more impressive than fireworks would begin. Our condo porch had a perfect view to the west, and although we couldn't see the ocean, our town was at a higher elevation that gave us a fabulous view of the lower mountains and hills along the beach.

ROLAND'S STORY

The earth spinning... orbiting the sun... planets and moons dancing together... all in the midst of an infinite number of other planets, stars, and galaxies. One had to wonder what incredible forces were at work. Was anything more magical than what we were experiencing just observing the Milky Way?

I pondered that in creating my own reality, in some small way, I was contributing to all this as one of the artists. Maybe in just taking the time to observe and appreciate its beauty, I was adding to the profound motion picture before me, owning a bit of a brush stroke in the masterpiece. I then ventured the thought that it was the collective thinking of all people as the extensions of the God/Universe that helped manifest the entire Universe itself. I had to wonder how many other solar systems had planets with life forms looking up into their heavens, contemplating the same theory.

After six decades of my life nearly passed, I had discovered who I was. Perhaps it was not entirely my true identity. But it didn't matter.

I knew I wasn't supposed to be "all that I am" right here and right now. I was here to specialize my own particular realm of experience with my own thoughts. Twelve weeks away from home had taught me an important aspect of my life. I knew that whatever my conditions were in my life, those conditions were up to me.

My view of the Universe had expanded considerably. More important, it continued to expand, my life being more about learning and growing than reaching some level of achievement. I also knew I would never stop. Yet my purpose of specializing remained. By doing so, I was adding details to Universal potential, and expressing my version of God's heaven on earth.

I had been happy every day for months now. But it wasn't about taking all the bad things and painting them with a coating of fake pleasantry. I sincerely enjoyed myself in all that I did. Quite

SIX MONTHS LATER...

simply, it didn't pay to be negative, so I had no use for it. And life was rewarding me with positive results for my effortless efforts, which is to say that being happy can be quite easy once you realize it's up to you.

It was Christmas Eve Day, and, as always, the kids were all coming for dinner, goodies and gifts. Barbara derived much of her holiday pleasure by making sure there was a stocking hanging above the fireplace for everyone who came to this dinner, and it seemed that we would grow by four people this year.

My son, Ty, would be here from Wisconsin, and with him, his fiancée. It would be the first time ever that all our kids would be together at the same time. Plus, there were friends joining us to add their joy to the festivities, and they were considered to be family as well.

Our traditions included appetizers and refreshments, whenever people started arriving; dinner; dessert; Christmas stockings filled with treats and small gifts; handing out packages with name tags; someone acting as Santa to sort out the pile; a rapid, rough cleanup; guitars; singing karaoke Christmas carols; and the inevitable yearly Nintendo 64 Tetris Challenge! This year would be much the same.

The sun continued to drop nearer the line of hills and mountains. As it did, the first stages of pink began mixing with blue and gold. Two by two, people were arriving. Gina and her boyfriend Mark; Katie and Megan; Kyle coming back from the airport with his girlfriend Natanya. Arms laden with bags and wrapped packages were unburdening themselves, their inventories being spread around various destinations in the front room and kitchen. Barbara was bouncing between the porch and the kitchen in order to juggle dinner preparations, and making sure that everyone had a drink and something to eat.

ROLAND'S STORY

Surprisingly, all of the family seemed to be arriving about the same time. The sky was a stage backdrop draped in curtains of ever-changing colors. In the middle of this growing party, I received a call from Ty saying that he and his girl were on their way and would arrive shortly.

Out of the corner of my eye I caught movement coming up the front steps. It was Kim and her daughter. Both of them had their arms filled as everyone else had, and I could see Kim balancing trays of what could only be her famous pot stickers, and who knew what else. I suspected cookies. Introductions started.

"Hi Kim!" I set my cup of hot chocolate down on the table and waved.

"Hi, Roland! Hi, everybody! Hi, Barbara!" She started setting things down so she could negotiate hugs. Barbara got to her first. As she finally was released by Barbara, she turned in my direction. She was in for a surprise.

I was standing. The week before, I had still been relying on the wheelchair. While Kim had been sharing hugs with Barbara, I had grabbed my new quad cane, and with some concerted effort, had achieved a standing position, left hand holding the cane. I was leaning a little to my left side, but that would have to do for now.

"Wow! Look at you!" That was all she could say.

I raised my eyebrows and shook my head as she started to come towards me. She paused where she was. As everyone watched, I slowly reached forth and planted the cane a few inches in front of me, and stepped further with my left foot. Then balancing on my left foot, I brought my right foot forward even with my left, and at the same time, repositioned the cane to match the distance. Again, I stepped with my left. They weren't perfect steps, and my body contorted a bit when I worked my right leg forward. But I

SIX MONTHS LATER...

was walking on my own, with a little help from a quad cane. I was standing two feet from Kim. It had taken me twenty seconds, but I had gotten there under my own power.

Kim closed the distance, and gave me a full standing hug. What happened next stunned her even more. As she held me there, I let go of my cane, and wrapped both arms around her, returning the two-armed embrace.

"Oh, my God, Roland! Your arm... you're hugging me back!" Kim exclaimed, and hugged me even harder, maybe to make sure I didn't fall. "Congratulations!"

"Thanks, Kim. And I mean, not just for the congrats. Thanks for believing in me, and helping me to see it, too." After a long time standing, for me that is, she helped me return to my wheelchair.

"You know, there's something to your method of healing. It's like you invoke some hidden power in people they don't realize they have. Now, I know what that power is. You're really onto something."

I saw a marketing plan forming in my mind, and wanted to incorporate it into her website outreach. "I had three calls yesterday. Two were patients from Lynfield that I kept in touch with, both wanting to get your number. And one was a parapsychologist doing research on psychokinetic healing. My doctor referred him to me, and told him he might find my case interesting."

"That's a weird coincidence, Roland." Kim said. "Someone from 'The Naturopathy Institute,' or something like that, wanted an interview regarding my use of laughter in healing therapy. I guess it's not a coincidence, is it? I think I'll check it out." We shared a chuckle.

"Very cool! How's your class doing, by the way?" The month before Kim had just completed a four week series of classes on ethnic dance exercise that she had dubbed 'Ethnocise.' Something she created herself.

ROLAND'S STORY

"Great! But it's three classes now!" Kim was obviously excited. "The lady who runs the center is apparently a member of an association of administrators, and she shared what we're doing at her facility. Two more senior centers have contracted!"

New possibilities were popping up all around us. Kim took a seat next to me and we continued talking.

"How about your web design? You getting work?" she asked.

"Yeah, I am." I replied. "But I'm not really trying hard to expand that business. I have other things in mind. I want to write a book."

"No kidding? Well, you'd be good at it. You have a way with words." Kim had read several of my recent blog articles on various subjects, including a new idea regarding what I learned by applying some of her techniques. It was getting some attention. Kim was even using the principle in her classes on therapy and healing. "You know, that 'mind-in-matter' concept is being received well, and people can easily understand it. I think it works."

"Me too. I'm going to have to write everything down with all its variables that we've determined so far. It's basically the same as other mental healing techniques, it's just that so many of them push the mind 'over' matter process, which suggests a struggle, and that caters to resistance. I believe I can remove the resistance, and write it so people will get it the first time."

"That's really great. Because in my classes, the mental healing technique helps people find the mindset to connect thought energy directly to their bodies."

Kim had been implementing a simple visualization technique that allowed people to engage a powerful positive mental attitude, and it was paying off. She had ever-increasing numbers of class enrollees in her new schedule. A major percentage of previous students were returning to continue to work with her.

SIX MONTHS LATER...

"Hey, what's that magazine thing you wanted to tell me about? You going to advertise in one?" Kim had mentioned something the other day, but we didn't have time to pursue it.

"Oh yes, Roland! I forgot!" Kim's excitement renewed as she took on this new subject. "A lady from 'Psychology Today' read a student review of my November class, and some of my other articles. She wants to talk to me. She's apparently creating a new magazine on holistic healing, and is interested in talking to me about publishing a column about my therapy experiences! She reached me through my blog! The first thing she asked me was, 'Are these actually true stories?' I said 'yes,' and she kinda freaked out. So she's going to call me Wednesday."

I sat there, and simply nodded my head in confirmation, and smiled. We had been talking for ten minutes straight, and neither of us had mentioned any challenges with no apparent solutions, but rather concepts having options with, as yet, undetermined choices.

It seemed that in a few short months, things had turned from trying times and stagnant progress, to beautiful days of abounding opportunities. I guess we had to admit that things were looking up.

"Dinner, everybody!" Barbara called.

"Want some help serving?" someone asked.

"I see you've got a new guitar!" New discussions.

"Did dad actually set up karaoke?" More chatter.

We moved into the house, wondering where we were going to put everyone. I thought it was a good challenge. We were happily extending the reach of our family unit.

I guess, regarding life's experiences, they're all good challenges. When I thought about the last nine months, it amazed me that so much could happen all within the time table of less than a year. During that time I had achieved much of my movement back. I

ROLAND'S STORY

wasn't back to normal yet. But as I thought about it, I had to ask myself, "What is normal?' and, "Did I really want to be normal?"

Through much adversity I had triumphed. We all had. And we were more excited about life than ever. Could that have happened if we had experienced a normal life this year?

Something told me that, by having what appeared to be a problem, I had been presented with an opportunity to take an alternate view of life, passionately desire more, and reach farther than I ever had before. So, had my stroke been a real problem? No. Not really. Just my mind playing a trick until I knew better.

Someone was knocking. Ty and his girl. There was so much going on. It was all good. As long as I could have value in the time that I spent, it was fine by me.

I looked beyond the doorway as Ty walked in, framed by a magnificent collage of changing hues of sunset, unique for this day, and never to be seen this way ever again. It filled me with something indescribable. I was learning to cherish the moment. It felt as if I was reading the message our ultimate skywriter was conveying to us during the continuous, never-ending flow of our existence. I was discovering the infinite essence of God that cannot be expressed in words.

I had an interesting thought just then. Here I was, almost at the end of my sixth decade upon this earth, finally knowing myself, and understanding my part in this world. I was happy with my journey, and felt no need to reach a goal of wealth or fame. Nor was I concerned with where my path might lead. I knew it was going to be beyond extraordinary. I was peaceful, and ready for the next challenge.

I had arrived. My real adventure had just begun.

SIX MONTHS LATER...

On August 23rd, 2018, Roland passed away peacefully from a final stroke, lovingly surrounded by his dear wife, Barbara, and their family. His legacy of "Expand Into Joy" lives on through his family and online friends across the world.

ROLAND'S REFLECTIONS

Roland S. Takaoka - husband, father, businessman, consultant, artist, musician, writer, friend.

I wear many hats. However, the ones that fit best and allow me to feel the most useful as a person, are the ones that are related to learning, teaching, sharing, and giving, and not necessarily in that order.

I consider it my responsibility to learn more, and acquire an ever-expanding awareness of truth. From there, it is my desire to teach others who would also like to know what I have learned, and share that which I consider available to all of us, truth. Artistic expression, music, and creative and descriptive writing, are all parts of what I have learned, and the essences of God-given abilities that we all have, I choose to explore in myself.

I am a devoted Law of Attraction Practitioner, and an eternal student of truth. Various parts of this book do indeed describe my philosophies regarding faith and Universal Law.

My wife Barbara and I are both ordained in the Universal Life Church, and conduct wedding ceremony officiant services. Most descriptions of historical time elements in the book are true, my Dad and Mom's comments, and my search for truth beginning at an early age. I am also an avid racquetball player, a fairly accomplished guitarist and vocalist, and have been designing websites since about 1995. I love my wife and our five kids. I have some amazing friends. We still strive to get together every Christmas Eve. We love our home in Orange County, California, where it's not too hot and not too cold, but just about as perfect as it gets.

Reaching the end of my sixth decade here on earth, I feel as though more of the Universe is awaiting discovery, and I plan to be the explorer for decades to come.

Part of that exploration will include my further recovery and return to full health, reading and writing many more books, and once again playing guitar, swinging the racquetball racquet, and spending as much time as possible with my wife, our kids, and friends.

A TIMELESS LOVE STORY

By Barbara Peeters

OUR MEETING

It was so powerful.

One day, I noticed this gentleman who kept coming into the store and he didn't really have a lot to buy. (Note: Barbara used to work as an Assistant Manager at a local CVS store.)

He just was hanging around. I went to my girlfriend and told her, "There's a man who keeps coming in the store. I'm getting the feeling God's telling me I'm supposed to help him."

I wasn't looking for a relationship. I was done. I even wore a wedding ring because I just didn't want to get involved. But this seemed like I was supposed to help him. I found out he was interested in

ROLAND'S STORY

me. I went over to the Starbucks nearby (where Roland worked with his computer), and he noticed me there. I would run in and out real quick. Then he would come through my line at work. We started a conversation, and he showed an interest and kept showing up in my life.

One day I went into Starbucks and the line was so long. It ended right at Roland's chair. Normally, the line doesn't go out into the lounge area, and that's where Roland used to work. He was looking at his computer and didn't notice me. I ran out of Starbucks because I didn't want to get involved with anyone. Then I just stopped because I knew there was a reason.

I walked back in, got in line, and said to him, "Excuse me, I think I'm supposed to introduce myself. My name is Barbara."

He just looked up at me and said, "Hello, I'm Roland. May I ask you one question? Are you married?" (I was wearing a ring!)

"No, I'm not," I said.

Then Roland said, "We will be talking." He was just floored!

Later, he told me that the night before he had been talking to God, and he said he was done. He was out of a divorce himself, and he was at the end of where he wanted to be in life. He was frustrated, sad and hurting.

Roland was talking to God, saying, "Please give me a sign of what direction I'm supposed to go." The next morning, I walked into Starbucks and introduced myself. It led into us going out.

When he asked me out, I told him, "I don't want to get into a relationship. My sister has been diagnosed with cancer. My whole family has been tested for a bone marrow transplant, and I'm the only one that's a match. So I'm moving up north to do a bone marrow transplant, and help take care of my sister. You may not want to go out."

A TIMELESS LOVE STORY

Roland said, "I want to go out anyway, just to get to know you as friends."

A SPECIAL RELATIONSHIP

So we did go out! Of course, we had the most amazing time.

At that same time, I looked for a job up north. My old boss had become a store manager, and she wanted to hire me and give me a promotion. It was already approved by the regional manager who knew me. I was ready to move.

All of a sudden, Roland asked me, "Where are you moving to?" I was going to move to the Bay area, outside of San Francisco, California. That's where my sister needed me. It's an eight hour drive, so it's not an easy drive back and forth to Southern California.

The more I got to know Roland, the more it seemed right. We were friends. We went around and did things together.

When he heard I was going to do the bone marrow transplant, he decided to take care of me, because if the person giving the transplant is not in good physical shape, it's an extremely dangerous procedure. I had gone through a divorce and a child custody case that was really nasty. My ex-husband was horrible, and I was down to 98 pounds. I was in no shape to do a bone marrow transplant, but I wanted to do it anyway. I'm 5'4" and I was a size one. That size was even big on me!

Roland decided to take care of me without hardly even knowing me! He gave me nutritional food. He helped me put on weight. That's the first time I found out about strawberries dipped in sour cream with brown sugar. It was wonderful! Then I helped him, because his daughter was going through a tough time. We became very close friends.

ROLAND'S STORY

I became healthier, did the bone marrow transplant, and ended up in the hospital. I got so sick, but I recovered. My sister didn't end up making it, but we tried. Because of the transplant, she did make it for another year. After the transplant, I talked to my parents and let them know the situation. I felt very good about Roland, but I said I was going to move up anyway.

"You don't even know if your sister's gonna make it or not," they said, "so don't move away from a future that might be right for you. Think of yourself."

They're such wonderful parents. I had told my boss in southern California that I was moving, and I already had the transfer. I was visiting back up north to settle things, and then, I just decided -- *I don't want to do this. I want to be with Roland!*

So I flew back down and went into my work. My boss happened to see me from his office. There was a window and it was upstairs. I started walking up, and he started walking down. We met in the middle.

"Did you change your mind?" he asked.

"Well, as a matter of fact I did. Can I have my old job?" I wondered.

"It's sitting here for you," he said.

So I stayed in southern California. Roland and I got together and continued on with life. We fell in love and had so many years together while he was not in a wheelchair. Before we even met, he had two strokes, but he recovered and was able to walk. He had a few signs of it, but he got back in and played racquetball and everything.

We were together about four years before we got married. All of our kids became like brothers and sisters. They love each other.

A TIMELESS LOVE STORY

AFTERWARDS... GROWING TOGETHER

We had a positive relationship through the entire time after his stroke because there was no other choice. Why be any other way?

I noticed other patients in the hospital didn't have regular family visitors. I know Roland got better care because I was there. They knew I'd be watching everything. They saw me bathing him and doing things. They knew the standard of care that I wanted for him was high. So they would make sure to take care of him.

I brought chocolates for the nurses, to show how much I appreciated them. You have to let them know your appreciation because they work hard. You'll receive better care and cooperation. Roland was there for a month and he shouldn't have been, but somehow, they figured it out.

I know that Roland was scared; he needed family. He had nights when he was crying but tried to never do it in front of me. He needed to know it was going to be okay. He needed to know someone cared enough -- that no matter what -- if he couldn't even use his body, someone would still love him. I think that was very important.

We laughed a lot, and I think that helps people heal on both sides. It was hard to watch him going through this. After a month, the doctors and nurses saw how committed we were. So, they figured out a way for insurance purposes to transfer him to rehab care.

He was there for two weeks and they would do a little physical therapy. I don't think it was good enough. Families really, *really* have to watch out for their loved ones, because they did not take good care of Roland.

A couple of times they were going to give him the wrong medications. Oh my gosh! Families need to know. You have to watch what they're doing in these homes.

ROLAND'S STORY

When the nurses weren't looking, I went and got a stack of towels and put them in a drawer near Roland. Every day, I would do a sponge bath for him. It was horrible. I couldn't believe it. I asked, "Did you have a shower? Did anybody wash?"

"No," Roland would say.

"Okay, we're getting up," I'd say. "We're going to bathe you." I'd have him hang his head over the sink, and I shampooed his hair and put clean clothes on him. I did all of his laundry. They didn't wash any of his clothes. So I would take them home, wash them and bring them back. I would be there first thing in the morning, making sure we would watch TV together, or we'd get on the computer. He stayed for a couple of weeks, and then they transferred him to a second place, which was supposed to be a higher level of rehabilitation. It was to be for a week, and it was 50 minutes away.

I still went every single day. We talked to the staff, and I said, "Please help with the basics: to transfer Roland back and forth, and help him walk or take a few steps. That's important." I was a bit disappointed, and so was Roland that they didn't help us. I would think helping Roland walk would be part of normal rehabilitation. They did a little bit of walking but didn't emphasize it. They were trying to get his arms stronger and straightened, which was not as important, because I could do that once he was home.

Instead, we needed him to be able to take a few steps. If he could take a step or two, he could get off the wheelchair, into the bathtub and onto the toilet, with me helping him… Luckily, at this point, I had learned how to use that belt around him, maneuver him, transfer him and move him around. I got better at that and he got a little bit stronger, so we were able to manage.

A TIMELESS LOVE STORY

ADJUSTING AT HOME

When he came home, for the first three weeks we did physical therapy. They sent in-home physical therapy a few times, and that helped us. Roland got stronger. I had a medical bar on the bed, so he could get in and out when he wanted. It was nice because he had some freedom, and he had the computer in the bedroom.

Roland couldn't get out of bed by himself when I had to go to work. Unfortunately, he had to get up early in the morning with me, but I would transfer him into the wheelchair. He had everything he needed to use the bathroom without getting out of the wheelchair. I would set up food, snacks, water and coffee. He had this pillow, and he would just sit at his desk and put his head back down to sleep some more. He had to sleep like that for a little bit. It was the only way, because I had to go to work and he couldn't get in his wheelchair by himself.

I had snacks in the bedroom. I made breakfast every morning. Then, I prepped lunch in the refrigerator, and he could get that out and put it in the microwave.

He could get around to get more food. He pushed the wheelchair with one leg and one arm. I pulled up all the rugs in the apartment. We took out a raised strip of wood on the floor, so he could roll a little easier. He could get on the computer; and see people all day long. We used to joke that he had a better social life than I did, which was wonderful. He talked to everybody, and had so many friends.

One person led to another. He was smart on the computer; he knew what he was doing. He figured it all out, and started doing shows through the computer. He could order the equipment he needed, and have it shipped to the house. He just set himself up. He did it immediately... the first week he was watching movies,

ROLAND'S STORY

emailing and calling people on the phone. He knew how to get on the computer, and see someone face to face. I know he did it with his daughter Gina and with a couple of friends. Within a week, he was talking to people on the computer, which was great.

I've always been a manager in my job, and I've learned you just take charge. You do what you have to do. The situation is the situation. There's no reason to be overwhelmed. There's no room for that. Roland didn't need me to be weak. He needed me to be a positive, fun person and help handle the situation. He was doing what he could do. I needed to do what I could do.

He was such a lovely man; we had such a good marriage and it was so positive. I'd try to get him dressed and his shirt would be all tied up, like a straightjacket. I was learning, and we would just laugh. I'd say, "Okay, let's try this again." I finally figured out how to do things, but it didn't overwhelm me. We figured it out. We might make mistakes, but that's not the end of the world. We got his shirt on eventually. We had food, I knew he could go back and forth, and he was taken care of every day. I told my boss that if my husband calls, I'm leaving that second and going home.

Roland was able to take a couple of steps, because the physical therapist was so good. But it didn't really last, because she couldn't keep working with him. He was able to raise himself up, take a step or two, pivot, stand up, move his legs and get into his wheelchair.

MANAGING THE STAIRS

When Roland had his third stroke, I let my parents know. When we first got him home, after a couple of months, I had to take him to the doctors. We had stairs down to the garage. We had to scoot up one step at a time! I'm trying to lift him up on each step, and he's trying to help, but he can't. We were both exhausted when we got up to the top of the stairs. We said, "We can't ever do that again!"

We both looked at each other, like what are we going to do?

I said, "I have no idea." Then we just laughed. Thank God, he was the man he was because we laughed at these hard situations. We didn't have any clue of how we'd figure it out. My parents bought us an electric lift chair for the stairs. Thank God they did that! I could get Roland in front of his wheelchair and onto the chair. He'd ride it down.

We had a second, old wheelchair in the garage. We transferred him to that temporarily, to get him into the car. Then I'd take his new, good wheelchair and transfer it down the stairs, put that in the trunk, and we could go and do whatever we needed to do. I would always carry the new wheelchair down and up. Roland knew I had a problem with my hip and knee; I needed to get knee surgery. So this was really hard for me. Roland came up with the idea of Bungee cording the wheelchair to the electric lift chair.

I figured out how to do that. Thank goodness! But we didn't get out as much as we wanted because it was a lot of work. We did go out to lunch or dinner, or we'd go shopping. When we did get out, that was really nice because we did exactly what married couples do to enjoy an evening.

ROLAND'S STORY

A MEMORABLE TIME

One time, I said, "Let's go to Starbucks." I love Starbucks. Always have. That's kind of my treat.

I don't go out to a lot of movies with my girlfriends, or shopping or anything. I treat myself to Starbucks. There was a Starbucks near us, and I'd stop there, and go on to work. I met these ladies at Starbucks and knew them all by first name. They knew me, my drink, everything. I was talking about my husband, how wonderful he is, and they said they'd love to meet him. He wanted to meet them too. So one of our outings was to Starbucks.

When we went, there was a long line. Roland was in his wheelchair and I was talking to him. We were laughing because we always had such a good conversation.

I noticed some drippings of cream on the floor, so I told Roland, "Excuse me just a minute, I'm just going to quickly wipe this up." I got some napkins, wiped up the floor, and threw them away. As we got closer to the register, and I noticed more drippings on the floor. I cleaned them up again, and saw where it was coming from.

"Your container is leaking," I told a gentleman.

Well, we got up to the front counter and there were two registers. I introduced Roland, and the ladies were thrilled to meet him. Of course, he was smiling and just the handsome, wonderful man that he is. The cashier said, "Your drinks are already paid for."

"What? What are you talking about?" We couldn't believe it.

They said, "Yes! One of the people in line paid for you. They want you to have something to eat too. What would you like to eat? It's all taken care of." Oh my gosh! Roland immediately asked, "Well, who is it just so we can thank them?"

The cashier told us, "They said they want to be anonymous."

So Roland yells out: "THANK YOU! THANK YOU! THANK YOU!" We still didn't know who did it.

One lady said, "This gentleman was so touched at the fact that you're in a wheelchair and you're being so positive. You and your wife are so loving, and she even goes and wipes up the floor! He just thought, what an amazing couple. You shared radiance all around you; he just wanted to do this for you."

"We never got to meet him. I think he probably wanted to see how much we enjoyed it. I'm sure he was around…. But you know, the funny thing is we had stuff like that happen often. We would go out to dinner, and people would come over and say hello. Roland was just very, very happy in life, which I think is amazing.

People would jump up out of their seats, away from their table to open a door. It was very nice. I loved being married to him. We had a wonderful, wonderful time together.

They said (at the hospital) that he'd be prone to strokes. Roland was taking his medicines. The doctors said, "You are going to have to

ROLAND'S STORY

be very, very careful. If you wanted to, you could go on a completely bland diet."

I would try and feed him healthy food. Then he'd say, "Okay, enough with the salads! I need some real food, you know." Every now and then, he'd get a burger or something, which was not healthy for him. He and I both believed that quality of life is more important than the quantity of years.

He loved food. We were very careful about his diet and I got rid of all the greasy stuff. But every now and then, he splurged. He'd say, "I enjoy some fun food every now and then. It's going to make my life so much better than me living longer and not being able to have what I love to eat. I'd much rather just enjoy life a little bit."

I don't think it really made that huge of a difference honestly, because we were really good about it. But it might've bought him another year. He was prone for strokes. It was in his family. Since he was in a wheelchair and couldn't move around, that made him even more susceptible to have another stroke. You've got to keep your body moving. I would rub and massage his leg. It would get red and swollen. I'd try and keep the circulation going, but it couldn't circulate. It was already in his family history.

It just was a matter of time. I guess I never had any idea that it could happen again.

ROLAND'S FOURTH STROKE

It had been six years since the third stroke. Every now and then on my days off, we would go out on the patio. I'd fix a meal and we'd eat outside, just because he was inside so much. It wasn't often enough.

He had been having these spells for about a month, where he would be a little bit dizzy and sick to his stomach. He'd have to take his glasses off and put his head down. I said, "This isn't a good thing; let's get you to the doctors."

I took him to his doctors. They said, "Maybe it's his glasses; maybe he needs a new prescription. But we want to make sure that that's what it is."

I asked, "Is there anything else going on?"

I was really concerned. It was happening on a regular basis, you know, often enough. Well, it wasn't his eyes. Nobody could figure out that he was on the verge of having a stroke. The doctors didn't see it. The regular general doctors set us up with an eye doctor. I made that appointment. But that took five weeks to happen! Then he went to a specialist.

"I don't want to just put this up to his eyes. I want to make sure he's okay," I said. He sent me to two different specialists. They did their tests. They said, "Everything seems fine." In the meantime, this was warning us that he was going to have a major stroke! But we didn't know. I set up another appointment for him. He was going in on the week after he passed away.

Roland was blessed because we knew if he had another stroke, he would have possibly lost his speech and more mobility. That's not the way Roland would have wanted to live.

REMEMBERING ROLAND'S FINAL DAYS

The night before the fourth stroke, we went out for a nice steak dinner. I usually wouldn't let Roland have steak because it's not healthy. But I said, "Okay, once a year, you can have a steak." So at least he thoroughly enjoyed it. That was wonderful.

It happened on Sunday, August 19th, 2018. I had worked half a day with my new job. Every day, I came home to have lunch. On that day, he was getting sick... throwing up... "This isn't good," I told him. "Do you want to go to the hospital? I think you should."

He shook his head no. "I don't know about this," I said, watching him in pain.

I sat with him for a little bit longer and knew I was not going back to work. Then he started not being very conscious. I called the ambulance around 3:00 in the afternoon. They picked him up, took him in, and then he went into ICU. He was there until Thursday when he passed away.

By the time I got to the hospital, he was conscious, but he had a tube down his throat so he couldn't talk. He couldn't really move. He was weak, but I could talk to him. I'd hold his hand and I'd say, "Squeeze my hand if you understand." The second he could, he'd squeeze my hand.

He was conscious for several days. I went home twice to get a shower, but I went right back.

My kids took care of my cat for me and I stayed the whole entire time.

His kids came to the hospital, and everybody got to say goodbye to him. The doctor said the only thing keeping him alive was the oxygen tube.

It was Wednesday morning, first thing in the morning, when the doctor came in and said,

"Do you want to keep him on the machines? We can do things to keep him alive. But he won't ever be able to speak again and he'll have to be tube fed."

I remember standing there with all three of his girls, and we're all holding hands. Roland was still conscious. I looked at him and said, "Baby, they're thinking of maybe taking the tubes out, but they don't know if you'll be able to sustain breathing or not. Squeeze my fingers if you want them to do that. Do you want them to put the tube back in?"

He shook his head no.

"Squeeze my fingers if you want me to make sure they don't put that tube back in," I said.

"Even if you're going to pass away." He squeezed my fingers. "I understand you don't want to live that way."

So when the doctor asked, "What do you want to do? You want us to resuscitate him if we take the tube out and everything?" The girls looked at me and said it's my call.

"No, he doesn't want that," I said. I already knew and the girls knew. "Is everybody okay with this decision? Because I'm willing to discuss it."

They all said, "We agree that's the way it should be. Dad wouldn't want that life." Then on Wednesday, at about 11:00 a.m., they took the tube out and the doctors started giving him morphine, because it was painful. He was conscious and everybody got to talk to him.

Roland was having a hard time; the doctors could tell by his heartbeat. I said, "Please just make him as comfortable as possible."

The doctor said, "It's just a matter of time when he'll pass away. He's not going to recover."

"Give him the morphine that you feel he needs," I told the doctor. Roland wasn't quite as conscious of course, because he was on morphine.

I slept next to him in the chair by his bed from Sunday to Thursday; I was there all night. I sat with him when they took the tubes out. After the "Get Well Roland" online program, I got to read off all the names of those who attended to him. So he knew. Then, on Thursday, August 23rd, 2018, he just left.

He always reached out and cared about other people. I know he's with all of us now.

ROLAND'S STORY

ROLAND'S MISSION…

- Always give to people.
- Don't think about what you're going to receive. You'll always receive no matter what, if you're doing the right thing.
- If you treat people right, if you're out there doing the right thing, if you're honestly doing it from your heart, it comes back to you. He was constantly helping people. They would call him, saying "This isn't working"… "I don't know how to do this…" "Can you help me with this?" And he would always help them, always.
- Be positive. There's no reason to be anything else, no matter what your situation. It doesn't help to do anything else.

#####

ACKNOWLEDGEMENTS

This book was possible through the loving support of a number of wonderful people.

Thanks To:

Aaron Avila, Ros Boundy, Michael Brown, Sandy Mosetick, David Goad, Renee Mollan Masters, Gregory Hubert, Teresa de Grosbois, Dr. Steve Taubman, Lea C. Jones, Bob Kauffman, Burt Kempner, Charmaine Hammond, Christopher Salem, Van Dai, Polly Vinograd, Bonnie Gibson, Dr. Josh Gilbert, Karin Spruill, Virginia Parsons, Mel Doerr, Shira Hunt, Donna Schwarzbach, Richard Kutok, Dr. Bob Bressman, Kathy Cress, Anna Birdy, September Dohrmann, Chad Coe, Lon McClure, Robyn Kole, Salud Salinda, Shari Goldberg, Linda Lamb, Jordan Sanders, Elaine Nieberding, Russell Dennis, Laura Marier, Lori Sica, James Demas, Jana Stanfield, Megan McDonough.

Grateful For Added Support:

Aaron Avila, Stroke TV
Ros Boundy
Ray Maczek, President The Standing Company
Virginia Parsons, Media Spotlight Marketing
Mark Alyn, Late Night Health Radio

ROLAND'S STORY

RESOURCES

Compiled by Lynn Sanders, these resources offer benefits in living life with positivity.

BOOKS

Altea, Rosemary, *You Own the Power*
Chopra, Deepak, *The Seven Spiritual Laws of Success*
Davis, Deanna, *The Law of Attraction in Action*
De Grosbois, Teresa, *Mass Influence*
Desai, Panache, *Discovering Your Soul Signature*
Dispenza, Joe, *Breaking the Habit of Being Yourself*
Emoto, Masuro, *The Hidden Messages in Water*
Hicks, Esther, *Ask and It Is Given*
Hill, Napolean, *Think and Grow Rich*
Jackson, Laura Lynne, *The Light Between Us*
Ruiz, Don Miguel, *The Four Agreements*
Shimoff, Marci, *Happy for No Reason*
Stringer, Jan and Alan Hickman, *BEE-ing Attraction, What Love Has To Do With Business & Marketing*
Taubman, Steve, *Buddha in the Trenches*
Tipping, Colin, *Radical Forgiveness*
Wattles, Wallace, *The Science of Getting Rich*
Weiss, Brian, *Many Lives, Many Masters*

RESOURCES

INSPIRATIONAL MUSIC

"A Whole New World" (Movie: *Aladdin*, Alan Menken & Tim Rice)
"Amazing Things" (Megon McDonough & Jana Stanfield),
    www.MegonMegon.com or www.JanaStanfield.com
"Be the Change" (Tiamo de Vettori)
"Circle of Life" (Elton John)
"Flashdance/What a Feeling" (Irene Cara)
"If I Were Brave" (Jana Stanfield)
"I Had the Time of My Life" (Bill Medley & Jennifer Warnes)
"I Say a Little Prayer" (Aretha Franklin)
"Look to the Rainbow" (Burton Lane, Musical: *Finian's Rainbow*)
"My Favorite Things" (Rodgers & Hammerstein, Musical: *Sound of Music*)
"Nothing Is Impossible" (Karen Taylor Good and Stowe Dailey)
    www.stowegood.com
"Precious Soul" (Karen Taylor Good and Stowe Dailey)
"Somewhere Over the Rainbow" (Israel "IZ" Kamakawiwo'ole)
"Somewhere Out There" (Linda Ronstadt & James Ingram)
"Stand by Me" (Ben King)
"Open a New Window" (Musical: Mame, Jerry Herman)
"We Are the World" (Michael Jackson & Lionel Richie)
"You've Got a Friend in Me" (Movie: *Toy Story*, Randy Newman)

WEBSITES

Stroke Online Support Program: www.stroketv.net, led by Aaron Avila and Jerry Wald.
Critical Thinking For Success: www.criticalthinkingforsuccess.com, Bob Kauffman.
American Stroke Association: www.stroke.org – 1-888-4-STROKE
Support Network: www.SupportNetwork.heart.org

ROLAND'S STORY

Sound Healing: www.vibrationallysound.com, Shira Hunt
Difference Makers Media: www.DifferenceMakersMedia.com
TUT's Adventurer's Club: www.tut.com
Keep Smiling Movement: www.Facebook.com/KeepSmilingMovement
The 100 Day Challenge: http://bit.ly/The100DayChallenge
The Big Dream Primer Online Program: http://bit.ly/BigDreamPrimer1

PRODUCTS

The Bemer: https://life.bemergroup.com. BEMER is a widely researched medical device, and known to enhance general blood flow in the microcirculatory system. Good circulation is essential for overall health and well-being. For details or to schedule a Bemer session, contact Lynn Sanders, Independent Bemer distributor at: sanders.bemergroup.com.

Standing Wheelchairs: www.thestandingcompany.com. The Standing Company custom-manufactures The Superstand Standing Wheelchair in three /1odels: Manual, Half-Power, Full-Power. Safe. Simple. Secure. FDA approved. A program of repeated passive standing in The Superstand Standing Wheelchair can improve a person's health by reducing urinary tract infections, reducing skin breakdown, stretching muscles/hamstrings/tendons, and improving respiratory capacity. Standing can improve opportunities for employment and increase independence. Frequent standing in The Superstand Standing Wheelchair is natural therapy; drug and pill-free. Proudly made-in-America (Saginaw, MI). It is time to stand up for yourself in The Superstand Standing Wheelchair. Call: 1-800-STANDING.

Learn more about creating legacy stories to make a difference and receive a free strategic story guide. Visit:
www.DifferenceMakersMedia.com.